Chinese Martial Arts Series 4
Fukien Ground Boxing
Nan Shaoling Leg Techniques

Written by Cai Chu-Xian (Tzai Tsu-Shien)
Translated into English by Mei Xue-Xiong (Mei Sue-Shiong)

SUGAWARA MARTIAL ARTS / JAPAN PUBLICATIONS

Chinese Martial Arts Series 4

Fukien Ground Boxing
— Nan Shaolin Leg Techniques —

福建地術拳

蔡楚賢 著
梅雪雄 譯

菅原総合武道研究所／日本出版貿易

Chinese Martial Arts Series 4
Fukien Ground Boxing
—Nan Shaoling Leg Techniques
　by Cai Chu-Xian
　Translated into English by Mei Xue-Xiong

©1993 by Cai Chu-Xian
All rights reserved, including the right to reproduce this book or portions thereof in any form without the written permission of the publisher.

Published by SUGAWARA MARTIAL ARTS INSTITUTE, INC.
　20-13, Tadao 3 chome, Machida-shi, Tokyo 194 Japan.
　Phone: (0427) 94-0972. FAX: (0427) 94-0899
　Edited by Tetsutaka Sugawara, Xing Lujian

First printing: September 1993

ISBN:0-87040-924-7
Printed in Japan

Overseas distributors:Japan Publicatiions Trading Co., Ltd.
P.O.Box 5030 Tokyo International, Tokyo 100-31, Japan.

Distributors:
UNITED STATES:Kodansha America, Inc. through Farrar Straus & Giroux, 19 Union Square West, New York, NY 10003. CANADA:Fitzhenry & Whiteside Ltd., 195 Allstate Parkway, Markham, Ontario L3R 4T8. BRITISH ISLES AND EUROPEAN CONTINENT:Premier Book Marketing Ltd., 1 Gower Street, London WC1E 6HA. AUSTRALIA AND NEW ZEALAND:Bookwise International, 54 Crittenden Road, Findon, South Australia 5023. THE FAR EAST AND JAPAN:Japan Publications Trading Co., Ltd., 1-2-1, Sarugaku-cho, Chiyoda-ku, Tokyo 101, Japan.

Preface

Fujian Ground Boxing is one of the branches of "Shaolin" boxing in southern China and is spread mainly among the people in Fuzhou, Fujian Province.

It is also called Shaolin Dog Style Boxing because of its unique methods. In 1979, it was recognized by the Sports Committee of China as a rare school in Chinese martial arts. As a kind of imitation school, Fujian Ground Boxing developed in the shape of a dog's movements such as running, punching, rolling, overturning, kicking, lying, dodging and feeling. You can practise in three levels, i.e. the upper-level, the middle-level and the lower-level, but the lower-level movements are the most superb of all, for they possess not only the first technique features of the southern Shaolin boxing, but also the unique ground skills which are celebrated for the various practical leg actions. With movements nimble and changeable, it really deserves to be called "the skills for seizing on the ground".

I have been learning Fujian Ground Boxing for about twenty years from the famous martial artsist Chen Yijiu, the president of Fuzhou Wushu Center. As a man with a career in the field of martial arts for more than a decade, I have developed some understanding of this technique. In order to carry forward Chinese martail arts, I would like to devote the systematized contents of the Fujian Ground Boxing to the enthusiasts of martial arts all over the world for studying.

The contents of the Fujian Ground Boxing include four sections: the basic movements, the shadow boxing, the paired practice and the essential lower-level skills for actual combat.

I wish to express my heartfelt thanks to Mr. Tetsutaka Sugawara, Sugawara Martial Arts Institute, Inc. Japan, who has given me so much invaluable advice and has done a great deal in the production of this book. Many thanks should be given to the friends in the world of martial arts for accepting this book and favoring me with their valuable suggestions.

Cai Chuxian
Vice-president of Fuzhou Martial Arts Association, China
Head Coach of Fuzhou Martial Arts Center

Contents

Preface

Chapter One: The Outline of Fujian Ground Boxing.......11

1. The Origin of Fujian Ground Boxing.......12
2. The Characteristics of Fujian Ground Boxing.......12
   1) Inclining the Neck Forward and Keeping the Head Upright.......13
   2) Arching the Back and Drawing the Chest In.......13
   3) Keeping Shoulders Lowered and Elbows Dropped.......13
   4) Bending the Waist and Keeping the Buttocks In.......13
   5) Bending Legs and Hooking Feet.......13
   6) Stretching and Shrinking in Turn.......13
   7) Tumbling.......13
   8) Piercing and Turning with Swiftness and Nimbleness.......13
3. Strength Training and Hard Exercises.......13
   1) Strength Training for Kicking.......14
   2) Strength Training for Hooking.......14
   3) Training for Iron Legs.......14
      (1) Prescription of Chinese medical herbs.......14
      (2) Prescription of Chinese medicines.......14

Chapter Two: The Basic Movements.......15

1. Lying Stance.......16
2. Single Bat Stance.......16
3. Double Bat Stance.......17
4. Crouching Bat Stance.......17
5. Shoulder Roll (Dog Rolls Like a Bead).......18
6. Backward Roll (Dog Turns Its Belly Over).......19
7. Piercing with Leg.......20
8. Fishing (Carp Up-jumping).......20
9. Straight Body Fall (Frog Pounces on Mosquitoes).......21
10. Serial Kicking (Rascally Dog Kicks with Its Heel Three Times).......21

11. Side Fall (Rascally Dog Lies on Its Side).......22
12. Backward Fall (The Leg towards the Sky).......22
13. Tiger Tail leg (Backward Kick).......23
14. Side Drop (Flying and Lying Buddha).......24
15. Cross-legged Drop (Thunder God Splits the Ground).......25
16. Butterfly Legs (Black Dragon Coils around a Pillar).......26

Chapter Three: The Shadowboxing.......27

1. Opening Form.......28
2. Smash Right Fist Forward in Bow Step.......28
3. Slap Instep of Right Foot.......29
4. Right Single Bat Stance.......29
5. Swing Right Leg Inward.......29
6. Kick Backward with Left Leg.......30
7. Shoulder Roll.......30
8. Jab Fingers Forward in Bow Step.......31
9. Stretch Palm in Bow Step.......31
10. Backward Roll.......31
11. The Leg Towards the Sky.......32
12. Left Butterfly Legs.......32
13. Right Butterfly Legs.......33
14. Shoulder Roll.......33
15. Front Kick with Heel.......33
16. Tiger Tail Leg.......33
17. Pierce with Right Leg.......34
18. Left Butterfly Legs.......34
19. Pierce with Right Leg.......34
20. Back Arc Kick.......34
21. Side Fall.......35
22. Carp Up-Jumping.......35
23. Front Tread and Side Kick.......36
24. Front Sweep.......36
25. Right and Left Single Bat Stances.......36
26. Back Arc Kick with Leg Bent.......37
27. Jumping Front Kick to Double Bat Stance.......37
28. Backward Roll.......37
29. Left Single Bat Stance.......37
30. Rascally Dog Kicks with Its Heel Three Times.......38

31. Kick Backward with Both Legs.......38
32. Side Drop.......39
33. Tiger Tail Leg.......39
34. Kick with Left Leg.......40
35. Straight Body Fall.......40
36. Left Single Bat Stance.......40
37. Kick with Right Leg.......41
38. Cross-legged Drop.......41
39. Hook and Kick with Legs.......42
40. Penetrate Ahead and Kick with Both Legs.......42
41. Carp Up-jumping.......42
42. Shoulder Roll.......43
43. Left Single Bat Stance.......43
44. Backward Roll.......43
45. Swing Right Leg Inward.......44
46. Hack with Right in Bow Step.......44
47. Closing Form.......44

Chapter Four: The Paired Practice......47

Preparatory Form.......48
Separate Palms Sideways in Horse-riding Step.......48
Fist-holding Salute.......48
Cut Forward with Both Palms in Horse-riding Step.......48

Chapter Five: The Essential Lower-level Skills for Actual Combat.......67

1. The Carp Wags Its Tail.......68
2. Golden Hooks Twist like Scissors.......69
3. The Rascally Dog Stretches Its Leg.......70
4. The Leg towards the Sky.......70
5. Bumping with the Knee.......71
6. The Boatman at the Helm.......71
7. The Ferocious Dog Blocks the Way.......72
8. The Agile Dog Lies on the Ground.......72
9. The Lying Dog Turns Over.......73
10. The Wily Hare Kicks with Both Legs (1).......74
11. Two Snakes Twine round the Neck (1).......75

12. Upper Kicking and Hooking (1).......76
13. Tiger Tail Leg (1).......77
14. The Boy Sits in Meditation.......78
15. Kicking the Golden Incense Burner from the Back.......79
16. Turning and Piercing with Left Leg.......80
17. Serial Kicking.......81
18. Separating Legs.......82
19. Burning Joss Sticks to the Heavens.......83
20. The Heavenly Dog Rolls a Ball.......84
21. Buddha Guanyin Descends to the World.......85
22. Lower Kicking and Hooking.......86
23. Threading a Needle.......87
24. Two Snakes Twine round the Neck (2).......88
25. Tiger Tail Leg (2).......89
26. The General Dismounts from a Horse.......90
27. Backward Hooking.......91
28. Frontal Kicking with the Hooked Foot.......92
29. The Rascally Dog Kicks with Its Heel Three Times.......93
30. The Agile Dog Turns Its Belly Over.......94
31. The Monkey Climbs a Tree.......95
32. Single-line Leg.......96
33. The Lying Dragon Wags Its Tail.......97
34. The Hungry Dog Springs on the Meat.......98
35. The Wily Hare Kicks with Both Legs (2).......99
36. The Black Dog Wags Its Tail.......100
37. The Rascal Takes Off His Boot.......101
38. The Bat Perches on the Ground.......102
39. The Drunken Dog Lies on the Ground.......103
40. The Old Man Pulls a Cart.......104
41. The Agile Dog Penetrates under the Crotch.......105
42. The Carp Tosses in Seething Waves.......106
43. The Dog Bites a Rice Dumpling.......107
44. Upper Kicking and Hooking (2).......108
45. The Celestial Binding.......110

Chapter One:
The Outline of Fujian Ground Boxing

1. The Origin of Fujian Ground Boxing

Fujian Ground Boxing is one of the rare schools in Chinese martial arts, with a long history. There is a legend telling us about its origin. It was said that in the Ming dynasty, there stood a White Lotus Nunnery opposite the Shaolin Temple in Quanzhou City, Fujian, China, in which the nuns were taught ground boxing for self-defense, and they kept the technique secret. But in the early years of the Qing dynasty, the rulers abused their authority and burnt down the nunnery and the temple, because the Buddhist nuns and monks had taken part in the rebellion against the Qing government in the hope of the restoration of the dethroned monarch. Therefore, the nuns and monks were forced to flee in all directions. One of the nuns with the title of "Master April" took refuge in a Chen family in Yongchun County, and was treated cordially as a member of the family. Deeply moved by the kindness from the old hostess, Master April passed on the technique of ground boxing to Chen Biao, the son of the family, as her repayment. After assiduous study, Chen Biao mastered it and regarded it so valuable a treasure that he did not let anyone else into the secret. From one generation to another, this technique was only handed down to their male descendants. This custom ended in the early period of the Republic of China, when one of Chen Biao's descendants Chen Ayin took flight to Singapore to seek asylum, for he had defended someone else against an injustice and killed a ruffian in his village. He then settled himself in Mr. Chen Yijiu's house. Being grateful to Mr. Chen Yijiu for taking him into his care, Chen Ayin later on taught Chen Yijiu the unique technique of ground boxing without the least reservation.

From his childhood, Mr. Chen Yijiu was ardently fond of martial arts and had early or late learnt a variety of them such as; Thai boxing, drunken boxing and dragon style boxing. After he discovered the true essence of the ground boxing, he applied himself to the study with great concentration and enormously enriched the contents of the technique. Thenceforth, he was held in high repute as "supernatural leg" by the people in southeast Asia because of his exquisite leg skills. Mr. Chen Yijiu left Singapore for Fuzhou in 1932 and has been living there ever since. From then, the Shaolin ground boxing began to spread far and wide in the vicinity of Fuzhou. Now, students of this school can be found all over and outside the province.

2. The Characteristics of Fujian Ground Boxing

As a kind of imitation boxing belonging to the Southern Shaolin Boxing system, Fujian Ground Boxing is noted for its agile and changeable footwork, as well as its fierce and vigorous fist technique. The essence of the technique is fully manifested in the lower-level movements with abundant leg skills. There is no lower-level movement without a leg action. In order to handle the technique skillfully, one should use his hands, legs and torso cooperatively. It requires that the hand acts as a rope, the body rolls as a ball, the waist works as an axle and the leg performs as a wheel. The basic rules are as follows:

1) Inclining the Neck Forward and Keeping the Head Upright

Keep your head naturally upright and do not sway it to either side while you lies on the ground. Incline the neck a little forward in order to look to the upper front.

2) Arching the Back and Drawing the Chest In

Relax your back naturally and draw the chest slightly inward, thus it is easier to bend the torso forward while falling. It may also keep the blood from rushing upward and guide the energy stream down to the acupuncture point "Dantian (lower abdomen)".

3) Keeping Shoulders Lowered and Elbows Dropped

Relax both shoulders and lower them. Keep both elbows naturally dropped and close to the ribs. While lying on one side of the body, prop the torso up on the hand and the forearm which are placed on the ground. As a saying goes: "Rely on the elbow to prop yourself up while falling, and do not separate elbows from ribs." You should meet this requirement in order to minimize the exposed vulnerable area of your body and protect your chest.

4) Bending the Waist and Keeping the Buttocks In

As the weight mainly rests on buttocks while lying on the ground, you should tuck the buttocks in and keep them taut. Meanwhile, you should bend the torso forward and maintain an arched body position in order to exert your skills more nimbly.

5) Bending Legs and Hooking Feet

When you perform the lower-level movements, legs are no longer the weight-bearing props, but the important parts to act. So you should bend your hips and legs so as to draw the knees close to the chest with your feet tightly hooked while lying on your back. Thus, you can efficiently exert your strength when you take an offensive with the legs.

6) Stretching and Shrinking in Turn

This requirement is specially related to the lower-level movements. Generally speaking, you should shrink your body tightly before stretching limbs to conduct an attack or defense. The right and left limbs also stretch and shrink in turn.

7) Tumbling

This refers to kind of typical ground movements which should be carried out skillfully and nimbly. These movements include forward rolling, backward rolling, passive dropping and active pouching.

8) Piercing and Turning with Swiftness and Nimbleness

You should stretch your limbs swiftly forward, backward or to the side while performing certain forms. When you return to the upper level from a lying position, you should roll skillfully, using your shoulders as an axis, as a wheel turns. The movements of the limbs will contribute greatly to bringing the torso up from the ground.

3. Strength Training and Hard Exercises

Since Fujian Ground Boxing emphasizes leg techniques, we must pay close attention to the leg strength training. The methods are as follows:

1) Strength Training for Kicking

Lie down on your side. Stretch legs alternately forward to kick something hard (such as a wall, a tree, a wooden man or a stake) with the sole of the foot. Do a thousand kicks every day, only exerting seventy percent of your strength with each act. On the one hand you do not have to spare your effort, otherwise the exercise will produce very little effect; on the other hand, you are liable to hurt yourself if you put forth too much strength. When you reach a high level, you will be able to knock your enemy down or break his leg with a single kick.

2) Strength Training for Hooking

Stand on a chair or other high object with one leg bearing the weight. Hang a heavy load on the hooked foot of the other leg and raise the leg till the thigh is level, then lower it. Do five hundred acts of this kind for each leg every time. You should increase the weight of the load gradually from five kilograms to a maximum of fifty kilograms. After one year's training, your legs will be strong enough to trip your enemy over with a single hooking.

3) Training for Iron Legs

Knock yourself on the shins with a stick of thirty to forty centimeters long and three centimeters in diameter. Hit lightly at first, then gradually increase the blowing force. Through a three-month's training, step by step, your legs will be strong enough to bump against a stake or tree trunk. Do one to two thousand acts of this bump every morning and evening for three years, then you may reach such a high level that you can break a stake of ten centimeters in diameter, or bend a reinforcing metal bar of four centimeters thick with a sweep of your leg, as Mr. Chen Yijiu did. Then, you will find it possible to stand the blow of a eight-pound hammer on the shins, without any pain. Therefore, you can not only strengthen your defense capabilities, but also increase the offensive effectiveness of your lower-level movements. If you utilize the following medicines as auxiliary materials, you will get remarkable effects much faster than usual.

(1) Prescription of Chinese medical herbs

Ginger, 1 kg. Roots of Chive, 250 g. Pine needles, 1 kg. Hair, 100 g. An ant nest on a tree. Crush the above materials and put them into a pot. Add 5 kg vinegar and cook until boiling. Then, pour the liquid into a bottle for future use.

(2) Prescription of Chinese medicines

Fresh manxing, fresh tuber of penellia, fresh chuanwu, fresh caowu, vomiting nut, root of Chinese wild ginger, root of herbaceous peony, Chinese angelica, Tibetan safflower, teasel root, rhizome of davallia.

Prepare 25 grams of each of the above materials and grind them into powder. Prepare 1 kilogram of white spirit containing 60 percent of alcohol and soak the powder in it for more than a week. Then, it will be ready for use.

Before you start the hitting exercise, dip absorbent cotton in the medical liquid and apply the cotton to wipe the area which is to bear the blow until the skin is heated up. Never wash your limbs with cold water after such an exercise. You should use hot water instead.

In addition to these three training ways, you had better apply other methods to improve the flexibility and the strength of your waist, wrist and fingers.

Chapter Two: The Basic Movements

There are sixteen basic lower-level movements which are of the most important in ground boxing. Only when you have mastered these well, can you understand the essence of ground boxing and apply them skillfully. During the former half of the first month, you should take one of the sixteen movements and repeat the exercise thirty to fifty times every day before you begin to review what has been learnt. In the latter half of the month, you should perform all the movements dozens of times every day. Thus, you will become practised with the basic movements in a month.

1. Lying Stance

This is a preparatory posture for an attack or defense while lying on the ground. Lie down on the right side of the body with the right buttock touching the ground, propping yourself up on the right hand and forearm. Bend the right leg at the knee and lift the lower leg with the sole of the foot facing upward. Hold the left leg sideways and off the ground with the knee sightly bent. Meanwhile, clench the left hand into a fist and swing it to the right front of the face, with the arm bent. Look to the upper front. (**Fig. 1**)

This is a right lying stance. To take the left form, posture yourself in the same way, only reversing "left" and "right". In doing the exercise, you can first perform the right lying stance, then sweep the left leg horizontally to the right from the front and sway the body to the left side, thus forming a left lying stance. Then, sweep the right leg in the same way to return to the right form. Repeat this action thirty to fifty times every day at the outset.

2. Single Bat Stance

Bend the right leg and drop to full squat. Bend the left leg and kneel down with the inner side of the lower leg and foot placed on the ground. Distribute the weight predominantly on the right leg. At the same time, the right hand rises, pausing above the right side of the head with the arm bent, the hollow of the hand turned up, blocking an attacking blow from above; while the left hand presses to the lower left. (**Fig. 2**)

When you squat on the right leg with the left knee on the ground, you form a "right single bat stance"; when on the left leg, a "left single bat stance". This form is a main link between lower and upper levels and is frequently used in the routine of the ground boxing. Perform the right and left single bat stance in turn and do thirty to fifty repetitions every time.

3. Double Bat Stance

Bend the legs to kneel down with thighs together and heels wide apart, placing the buttocks, the inner sides of the lower legs and feet on the ground. Meanwhile, hold both hands separately in front of the shoulders with the hands crooked at wrists and the arms extremely bent and against the ribs. The hollows of the hands face downward and the fingers point outward. **(Fig. 3)**

When practising the double bat stance, take the static posture first, then fall down suddenly into the stance from a standing position. Finally, you can jump up and then drop into the stance.

4. Crouching Bat Stance

Sit down on the right buttock, with the right leg bent and folded tightly in front of the body and the left leg bent and held sideways, placing the outer side of the right leg and the inner side of the left leg on the ground. Hold the right fist by the right side of the waist with the hollow of the fist facing upward. Place the left palm in front of the right shoulder with the arm bent, the fingers pointing upward and the hollow of the hand facing rightward. **(Fig. 4)**

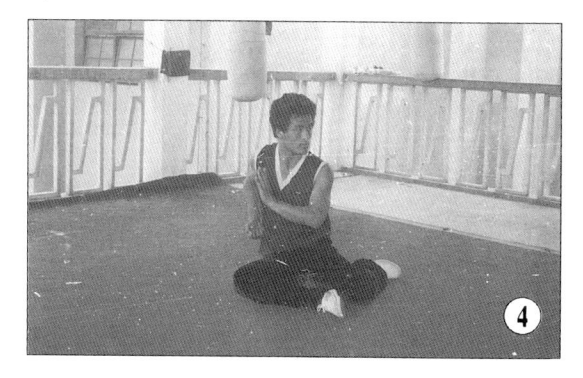

This is a right crouching bat stance. You can reverse "left" and "right" to form a left crouching bat stance. When you fail in upper-level fighting, you can suddenly drop into a crouching bat stance and then apply the ground techniques to attack or defend effectively. The crouching bat stance is usually followed by leg movements. You should practise this form on either side.

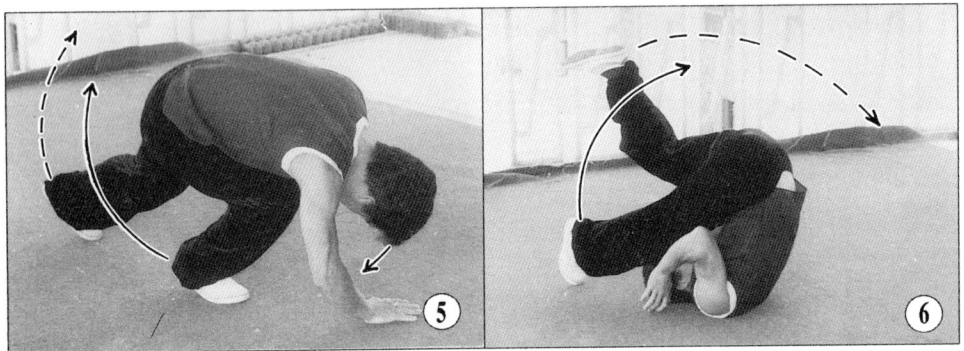

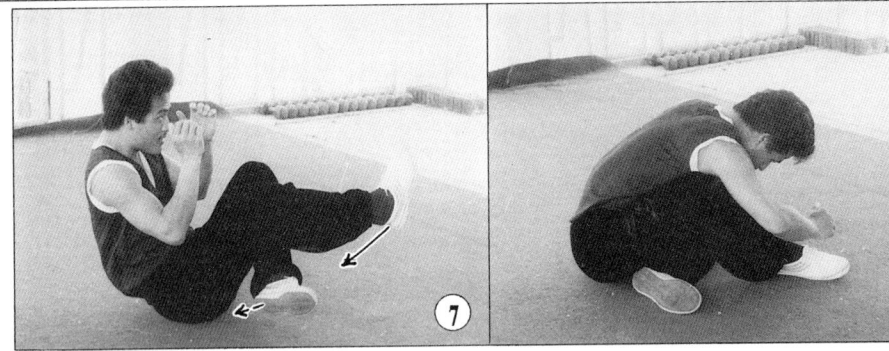

5. Shoulder Roll (Dog Rolls Like a Bead)

1) Step forward with the right foot. Bend legs and bow forward with the heel of the left foot raised. Place the right hand on the ground in front of the body with the arm bent.. (**Fig. 5**)

2) Bow the head and tuck the chin tightly in. The body then rolls forward with the right shoulder and the back of the torso touching the ground in succession. Place the left hand on the ground and swing the legs up when the body rolls. (**Fig. 6**)

3) The body continues to roll forward, with both hands drawn to the front of the chest. (**Fig. 7**)

4) As the feet land on the ground, sit up with the head going upward and forward, the arm hanging down naturally. Then stand up. (**Fig. 8**)

The shoulder roll is one of the fundamental movements for attack and defense in ground boxing, and you can perform it smoothly and swiftly only through frequent exercises. Do thirty repetitions every time.

6. Backward Roll (Dog Turns Its Belly Over)

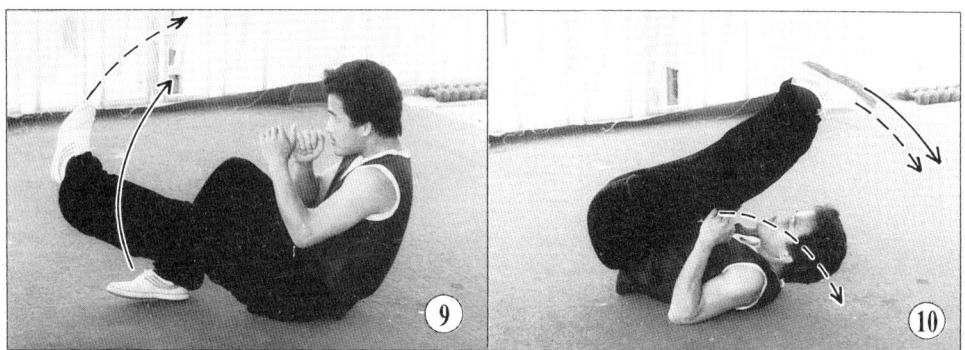

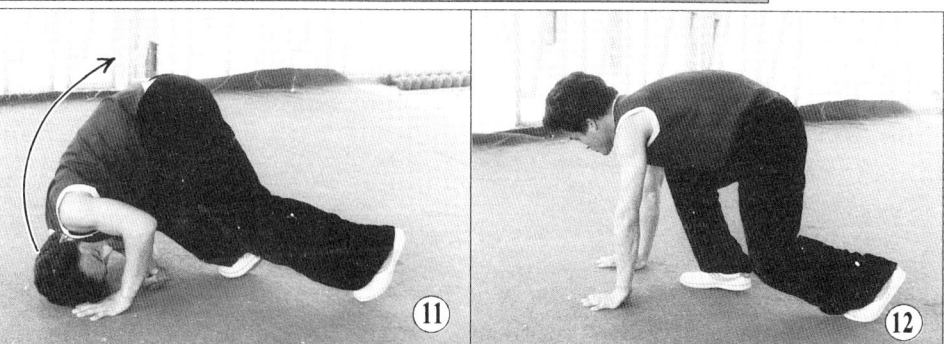

1) Bend the left leg and lower the body. Extend the right leg forward with its foot hooked up. The body then falls down with the buttocks landing on the ground. Hold both arms in front of the chest with the elbows bent. **(Fig. 9)**

2) While the body lies supine on the ground, the left leg stretches forward. Then, both legs together swing in a vertical arc upward. **(Fig. 10)**

3) The body continues to roll backward with the head bowed and the chin tucked in close to the chest. When the body turns over, place both hands on the ground. Both legs then land on the ground with the feet slightly separated. **(Fig. 11)**

4) Straighten both arms to prop the torso up. **(Fig. 12)**

This movement is as important as the shoulder roll. Exercise yourself until you can complete it smoothly and swiftly. Do thirty repetitions every time.

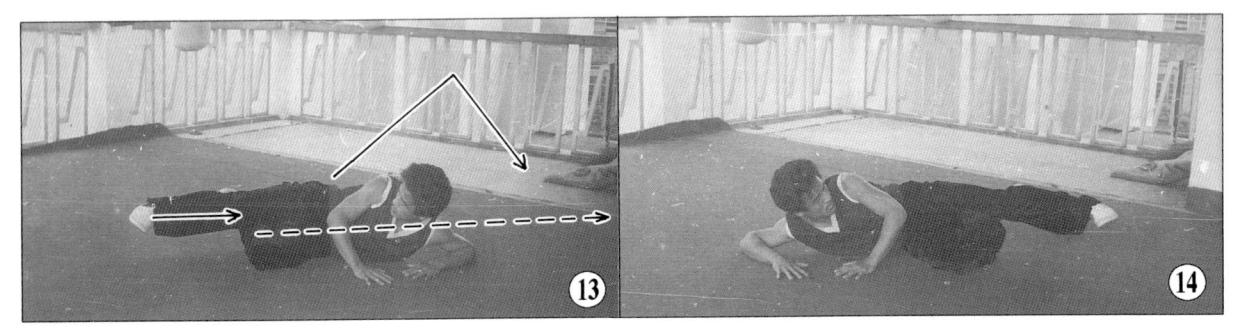

7. Piercing with Leg

1) Lie down on the left side of the body with the left bent and folded. Place both hands and the left forearm on the ground to prop the torso slightly up. Meanwhile, the right leg kicks horizontally sideways, with force concentrated on the outer edge of the foot. Fix your eyes on the right foot. (**Fig. 13**)

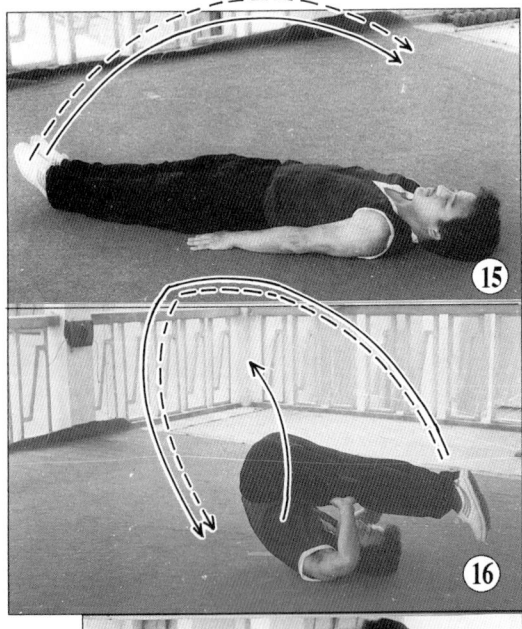

2) Without any pause, both hands push the ground to lift the body up. The torso then sways to the right. After that, repeat the same movement as described in Fig. 13, only reversing "left" and "right". (**Fig. 14**)

Piercing with leg is an effective method to launch a long distance attack. You can apply it to destroy your opponent's stance easily. You should perform the movement swiftly and powerfully. Do thirty repetitions every time.

8. Fishing (Carp Up-jumping)

1) Lie on your back with your legs together and toes pointed. Place both arms on the sides of the body with palms against the ground. Look upward. (**Fig. 15**)

2) Roll backward slightly, supporting yourself with the back. Meanwhile, bend the hips, swinging both legs upward and folding them up close to the torso. Simultaneously, place both hands separately on the thighs, with the arms bent. (**Fig. 16**)

3) Without any pause, exert the strength

20

of the muscles on your back and waist to swing both legs upward, with both hands pushing the thighs forcefully so as to quicken the legs' motion. As the torso comes up with the hips straightened, both legs continue to press down swiftly with the knees slightly bent, to land on the balls of the feet. The movement ends when you stand up with both arms naturally bent and held in front of the torso to keep balance. **(Fig. 17)**

This is a transitional movement from the lower to the upper level. You should complete it swiftly and skillfully. At least forty repetitions are needed for each practice. In order to avoid injury, you had better get someone else to support you by the waist while you are doing this exercise, especially at the outset.

9. Straight Body Fall (Frog Pounces on Mosquitoes)

1) Stand upright with the feet together. Bend both arms and hold the fists in front of the shoulders, with the hollows of the fists facing the torso. Look forward. **(Fig. 18)**

2) Lean forward and fall down, keeping the body straight as a stone tablet, landing with the outer sides of the forearms to support the body. **(Fig. 19)**

This is a typical tumbling movement for protecting yourself against injuries when you are knocked down by your opponent. Ten to twenty repetitions are needed for each practice.

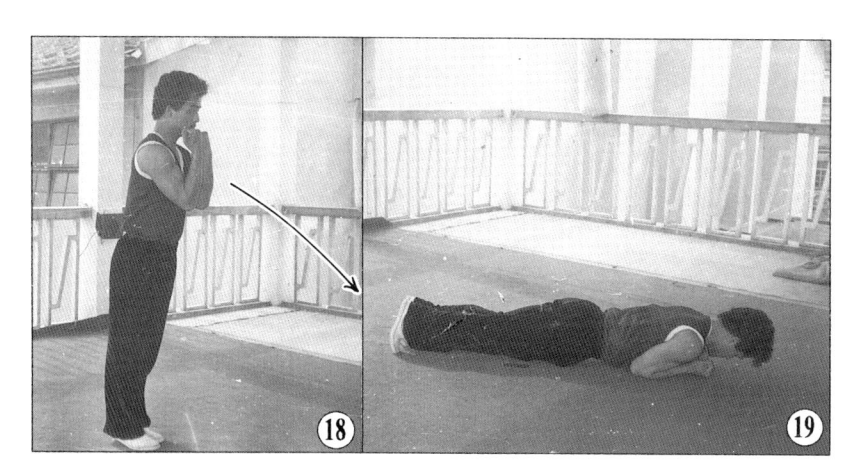

10. Serial Kicking (Rascally Dog Kicks with Its Heel Three Times)

1) Lie on your back and hold both fists in

21

front of the chest with the arms bent. Bend the legs and fold them up close to the torso. The right leg then kicks forcefully upward with its heel. Bow the head slightly and look to the upper front. (**Fig. 20**)

2) Without any pause, as the right leg drops with the knee bent, the left leg kicks forcefully upward with its heel. (**Fig. 21**)

3) Without any pause, as the left leg drops with its knee bent, the right leg kicks forcefully upward with its heel. (**Fig. 22**)

This is a powerful lower-level method for attack or defense. You should perform the kicks swiftly and vigorously, taking the opponent's belly or crotch as your target. At least one hundred repetitions are needed for each practice.

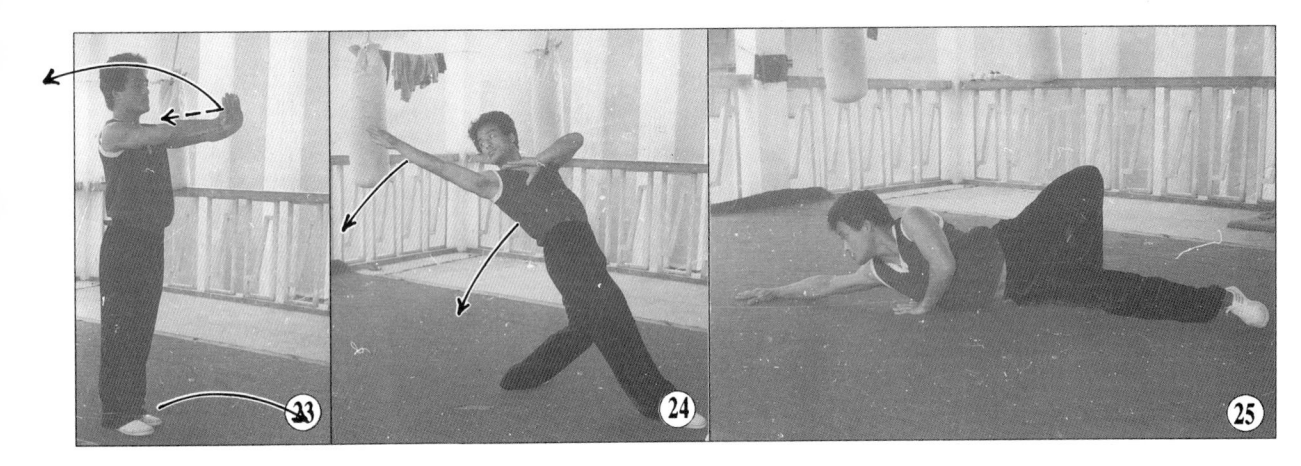

11. Side Fall (Rascally Dog Lies on Its Side)

1) Stand upright with the feet together. Stretch both arms forward with the wrists crossed, the fingers pointing upward and the hollows of the palms facing obliquely outward. (**Fig. 23**)

2) Lean backward and turn the torso slightly to the right with the left leg bent and the right leg stretched forward. At the same time, the right arm swings to the right rear with the hollow of the hand facing downward; while the left hand moves to the front of the right shoulder with the arm bent. Fix your eyes on the right hand. (**Fig. 24**)

3) Bend the left leg to the full extent and lower the body while the torso continues to turn about 90 degrees to the right. Then, fall sideways down with the outer edge of the right foot sliding forward on the ground. While landing, place both hands and the right forearm on the ground to support the body, keeping the right arm straight and the left arm bent. (**Fig. 25**)

This is an effective method for safe dropping when you are thrown into passivity in upper-level combat or when you are tripped by your opponent.

12. Backward Fall (The Leg towards the Sky)

1) Stand upright with the feet together. Then, bend legs and drop to half squat.

Meanwhile, smash the right fist down. The left palm meets the back of the right fist in front of the abdomen, with both arms bent. **(Fig. 26)**

2) Shift the weight onto the slightly bent left leg. As the body leans backward, the right leg rises and kicks forward with its heel. Meanwhile, stretch both arms sideways at shoulder level, palms facing outward. Look straight ahead. **(Fig. 27)**

3) Fall backward with the chin tucked in, landing on the ground with the back and the shoulders. Straighten the left hip and bend the left leg at the knee with the ball of the foot pressing on the ground so as to prop the waist and the buttocks off the ground. Simultaneously, the right leg continues to kick upward with its heel. Look upward. **(Fig. 28)**

This is an effective attacking method which can be applied when you are forced to fall backward.

13. Tiger Tail leg (Backward Kick)

1) Kneel down on the left knee and prop the torso by placing both hands on the ground, with both arms bent. Simultaneously, the right leg kicks with its heel towards the upper rear. Turn the head to the right and look in the direction of the right foot. **(Fig. 29)**

2) Bring the right leg down to a kneeling position. Then, push the ground with the hands and turn the body swiftly round to the right to about 180 degrees, using the right knee as an axis. After that, the left leg kicks with its heel towards the upper rear, prop the torso by placing both hands on the ground again. Turn the head to the left and look in the direction of the left foot. **(Fig. 30)**

This is also a powerful lower-level method to subdue your enemy or protect yourself. Do the practice on either side and make thirty to fifty repetitions every time.

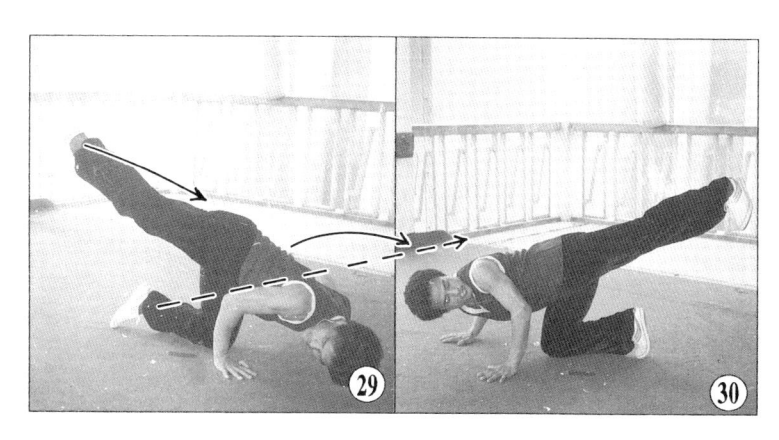

14. Side Drop (Flying and Lying Buddha)

1) The right leg takes a step forward with the toes turned outward. Shift the weight forward with the heel of the left foot raised. As the right hand swings forward with the hollow of the palm facing upward, the left hand comes up and then presses upon the crook of the right arm with the hollow of the palm facing downward. Look forward. (**Fig. 31**)

2) As the left leg swings up with the knee bent, the right leg stamps the ground forcefully to jump up. (**Fig. 32**)

3) As the body rises in the air, turn the torso to the right and raise the right leg with the knee bent. The left leg kicks horizontally sideways with the toes turned in and force concentrated on the outer edge of the foot. At the same time, the right hand draws back to the front of the chest; while the left palm pushes to the left side, force concentrated on the little-finger side of the hand. (**Fig. 33**)

4) Incline the torso to the right while the body is still in the air. Then, drop down with the right leg bent and the left leg stretched out. While landing, the outer side of the right leg, the sole of the left foot, the right forearm and both the palms touch the ground at the same time. (**Fig. 34**)

As this is a very difficult dropping movement after a jump, you should perform it accurately and had better carpet the ground for fear of injuries. You should practise the drop over and over again assiduously in order to have a good grasp of the complicated technique.

15. Cross-legged Drop (Thunder God Splits the Ground)

1) Stand with the feet a step width apart. Bend both legs slightly and keep the weight predominantly on the ball of the right foot. Turn the torso to the right and hold the right arm on the right side at shoulder side at shoulder level with the hand clenched into a fist. Hold the left hand in front of the chest with the arm bent. Fix your eyes on the right fist. (**Fig. 35**)

2) As the left arm swings downward, passing before the abdomen, and then to the left, swing the left leg sideways up with the knee bent, and stamp the ground quickly and forcefully with the right leg to jump up into the air. Turn the body about 270 degrees to the left through the jump. (**Fig. 36**)

3) The body continues to turn about 90 degrees to the left and leans to the left side; while the right leg swings upward and around until it presses down to the right side. The body then drops down with both legs crossed like a pair of scissors. While landing, the outer side of the left leg and both the forearms touch the ground at the same time, keeping the arms bent. Look to the right. (**Fig.37**)

This dropping movement is as difficult and complicated as the side drop. So you had better practise it on the carpet-covered ground to avoid injuries.

16. Butterfly Legs (Black Dragon Coils around a Pillar)

1) Lie on the right side of the body. Place both hands and the right forearm on the ground to prop yourself up. Bend the right leg with its outer side touching the ground. Fix your eyes on the left foot. **(Fig. 38)**

2) Lie on your back while the left leg sweeps horizontally counterclockwise, passing before the face, then to the left. The right leg follows to sweep in a horizontal circle to the left. Prop the buttocks and the waist up and keep the legs naturally apart while they are twisting in the air. **(Fig. 39)**

3) Without any pause, turn the body to a left lying position with both hands and the left forearm placed on the ground to support the torso, keeping the arms bent. At the same time, bend the left leg with its outer side touching the ground, and stretch the right leg above the left one with its toes resting on the ground. Fix your eyes on the right foot. **(Fig. 40)**

This is a "right butterfly legs". If you first lie on the left side of the body and swing the legs horizontally clockwise in succession (the right leg goes before the left leg follows), you are performing a "left butterfly legs". The "butterfly legs" is one of the essential methods of the ground boxing. Through continuous exercise, you can certainly improve your flexibility and enhance your ability to turn and roll freely and skillfully. Practise both the right form and the left form for about fifty times in each workout.

Chapter Three: The Shadowboxing

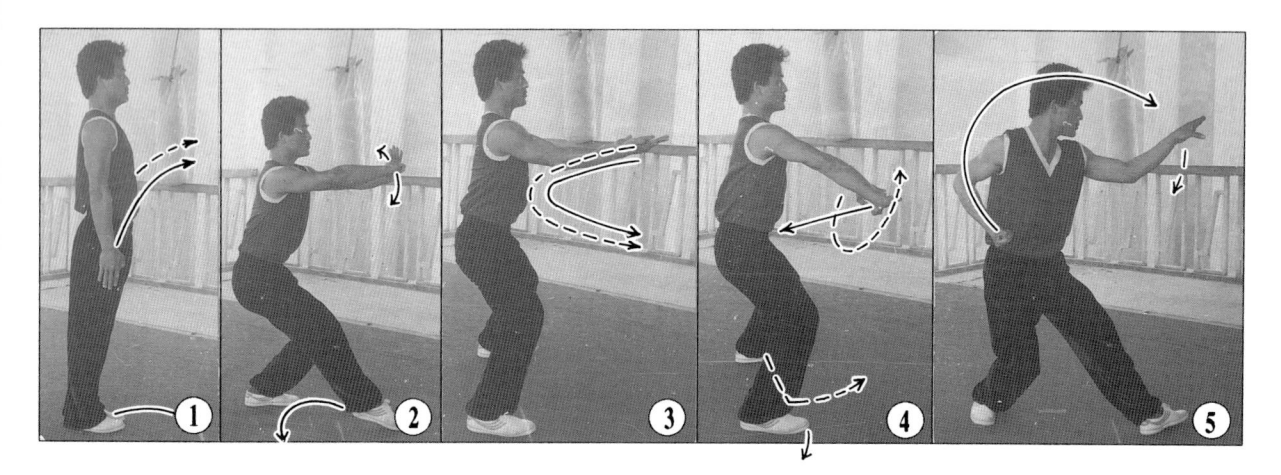

1. Opening Form

1) Stand upright with the feet together, both arms hanging down naturally with the palms close to the outer sides of the thighs. Look straight ahead. (**Fig. 1**)

2) Bend the left leg and move the right foot a step forward with its toes resting on the ground to form a right empty step. Meanwhile, the right hand clenches into a fist. The right fist and the left palm then push forward from beside the waist, with the left palm adhering to the right fist, the hollow of the palm facing rightward. (**Fig. 2**)

3) Draw the right foot back and move it to the right side about a step-width apart from the left, with both feet parallel to each other, so as to form a horse-riding step. At the same time, open the right fist. Both hands then separate sideways with the arms slightly bent and the hollows of the hands facing upward. (**Fig. 3**)

4) Without any pause, draw both hands to the sides of the waist, then push them forward with the hollows of the hands turned down and fingers pointing inward. Keep the arms naturally bent and a shoulder-width apart from each other. (**Fig. 4**)

2. Smash Right Fist Forward in Bow Step

1) The left leg takes a step forward with the toes of the right foot turned outward. At the same time, the left hand draws slightly backward, then moves in a small circle passing before the abdomen, finally makes a grab to the front, keeping the four fingers together and the thumb apart from the four. The right hand clenches into a fist and withdraws to the right side of the waist in the meantime. (**Fig. 5**)

2) Without any pause, shift the weight forward with the left leg bent at the knee and the right leg straightened to form a left bow step. At the same time, the right fist rises with the elbow bent, then swings to the front, striking the opponent on the head, with force concentrated on the back of the fist; while the left hand presses down to the front of the abdomen with the arm bent. **(Fig. 6)**

3. Slap Instep of Right Foot

As the weight is shifted forward onto the left leg, the right leg kicks forward and upward with the knee and the ankle straightened. The right fist opens and then slaps the instep of the foot in front of the face. The left hand moves slightly outward in the meantime. **(Fig. 7)**

4. Right Single Bat Stance

Without any pause, lower the right foot and place it to the right rear on the ground. Turn the torso to the right and crouch down with the inner side of the left lower leg and foot placed on the ground to form a right single bat stance. Thump the ground with both hands when you bow down. Turn the head to look to the lower left. **(Fig. 8)**

5. Swing Right Leg Inward

Stand up and turn the torso to the left. Shift the weight onto the slightly bent left leg. Meanwhile, the right leg swings in a fan-shaped curve, first sideways up, then inward and to the left. The left hand swings up and slaps the sole of the right foot in front of the face. Simultaneously, the right hand clenches into a fist and moves to the right side of the waist. Fix your eyes on the right foot. **(Fig. 9)**

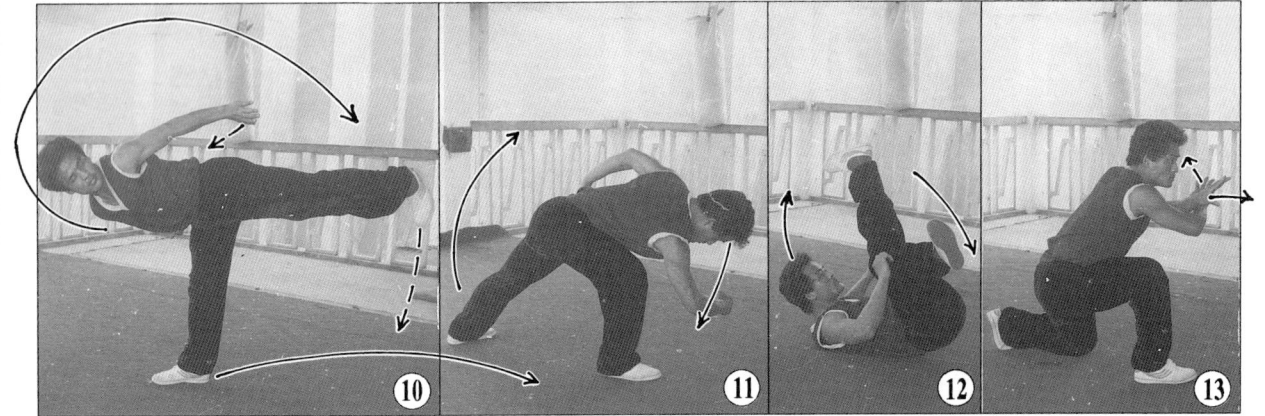

6. Kick Backward with Left Leg

As the right lg swings down and lands on the ground to bear the weight, the body turns about 270 degrees to the left and bows down until the torso is almost level. Meanwhile, the left leg kicks backward with its heel. The left hand swings upward while the left leg kicks. **(Fig. 10)**

7. Shoulder Roll

1) As the left foot lands on the ground, the body turns to the left. Then, step forward with the right foot and bend the torso forward. At the same time, the left hand draws back to the left side of the waist, while the right hand moves forward with the forearm crosswise in front of the right knee. **(Fig. 11)**

2) Without any pause, the body rolls forward with the right shoulder and the back of the torso touching the ground in succession. **(Fig. 12)**

3) As the body turns over, place the right foot on the ground with the knee bent, and kneel down on the left knee. The torso comes up and leans slightly forward. Both hands cross in front of the chest with the arms bent, the left hand on top. **(Fig. 13)**

8. Jab Fingers Forward in Bow Step

Step forward with the right foot. Bend the right leg at the knee and straighten the left leg to form a right bow step. At the same time, with the forefinger and the middle finger stretched together and the other three clenched in the hollow of the palm, jab the two fingers into the imaginary enemy's eye; while the left hand swings to the left rear with the hand crooked at the wrist. Fix your eyes on the right fingers. **(Fig. 14)**

9. Stretch Palm in Bow Step

1) As the torso turns to the left, the left foot takes a step to the right from behind the right foot, with the ball placed on the ground to form a cross-legged stance. At the same time, the left palm swings to the front of the right shoulder, with the wrist dropped and the hollow of the palm facing rightward; while the right hand changes into a normal palm and draws back to the front of the abdomen, with the hollow of the palm facing upward. Look to the right. **(Fig. 15)**

2) Without any pause, the right foot takes a big step to the right. Bend the right leg at the knee and straighten the left leg to form a right bow step. As the torso leans to the right, the right hand stretches out to the lower right with the hollow of the palm facing upward, so as to seize the enemy by the crotch. Simultaneously, the left hand swings upward and pauses overhead to block a blow from above, with the arm bent and the hollow of the palm facing upward. Fix your eyes on the right palm. **(Fig. 16)**

10. Backward Roll

1) Shift your weight backward and fall down on your back. As the body falls, bend the left leg and draw the knee close to the chest. The right leg swings upward with the knee straightened. Draw both hands backward in the meantime. **(Fig. 17)**

2) The body continues to roll backward. After you turn over, place the left foot on the ground with the knee bent to its full extent and kneel down on the right knee, forming a left single bat stance. Both palms are placed on the ground too. with the arms straightened. **(Fig. 18)**

31

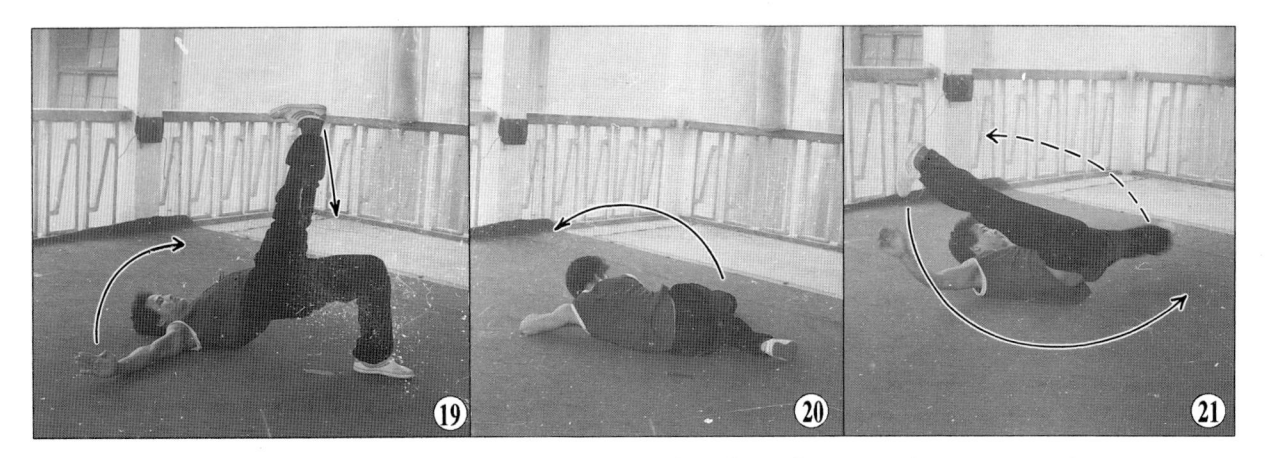

11. The Leg Towards the Sky

Stretch both arms sideways and fall backward, landing with the shoulders and the arms touching the ground. Meanwhile, straighten the left hip and bend the left leg at the knee, with the ball of the left foot pressing on the ground so as to prop the waist and the buttocks off the ground. The right leg kicks forcefully upward with its heel while the body falls. Look upward. **(Fig. 19)**

12. Left Butterfly Legs

1) Turn the body to a left lying position with both hands and the left forearm placed on the ground to support the torso, keeping the arms bent. At the same time, bend the left leg with its outer side touching the ground, and stretch the right leg above the left one with its toes resting on the ground. **(Fig. 20)**

2) Lie on your back while the right leg sweeps horizontally clockwise, passing before the face, then to the right. The left leg follows to sweep in a horizontal circle. Prop the buttocks and the waist up while both legs are twisting in the air. **(Fig. 21)**

3) Without any pause, turn the body to a right lying position with both hands and the right forearm placed on the ground to support the torso, keeping the arms bent. At the same time, bend the right leg with its outer side touching the ground, and

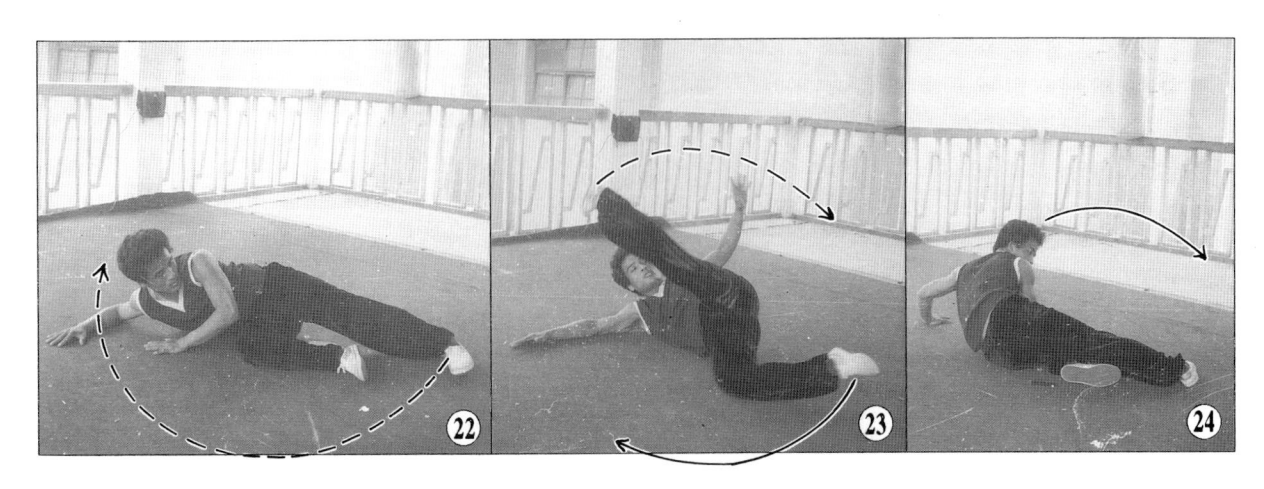

stretch the left leg above the right one with its toes resting on the ground. Turn the head to look to the upper left. (**Fig. 22**)

13. Right Butterfly Legs

1) Lie on your back while the left leg sweeps horizontally counterclockwise, passing before the face, then to the left. The right leg follows to sweep in a horizontal circle. Prop the buttocks and the waist up and keep the legs naturally apart while they are twisting in the air. (**Fig. 23**)

2) Without any pause, turn the body to a left lying position with both hands placed on the ground to support the torso, keeping the arms bent. At the same time, bend the left leg with its outer side touching the ground, and stretch the right leg above the left one with its toes resting on the ground. Turn the head to the right. (**Fig. 24**)

14. Shoulder Roll

1) The torso comes forward by pushing the ground with both hands. Squat on the fully bent right leg and kneel down on the left knee. Hold the right hand crosswise in front of the chest with the arm bent, and keep the left hand under the right arm. (**Fig. 25**)

2) The body rolls forward with the right shoulder and the back of the torso touching the ground in succession. (**Fig. 26**)

15. Front Kick with Heel

1) After you turn over, stand up on the slightly bent left leg with the ball of the right foot placed behind on the ground. Meanwhile, hold both arms obliquely forward at shoulder level, with the elbows naturally bent and the hollows of the hands facing obliquely outward. Look straight ahead. (**Fig. 27**)

2) As the weight is shifted forward onto the left leg with the torso leaning slightly backward, the right leg kicks with its heel to the upper front. (**Fig. 28**)

16. Tiger Tail Leg

Lower the right foot and turn the body round to the left. Then, kneel down on the right knee, placing both hands on the ground to support the torso. Meanwhile, the left leg kicks with its heel to the upper

33

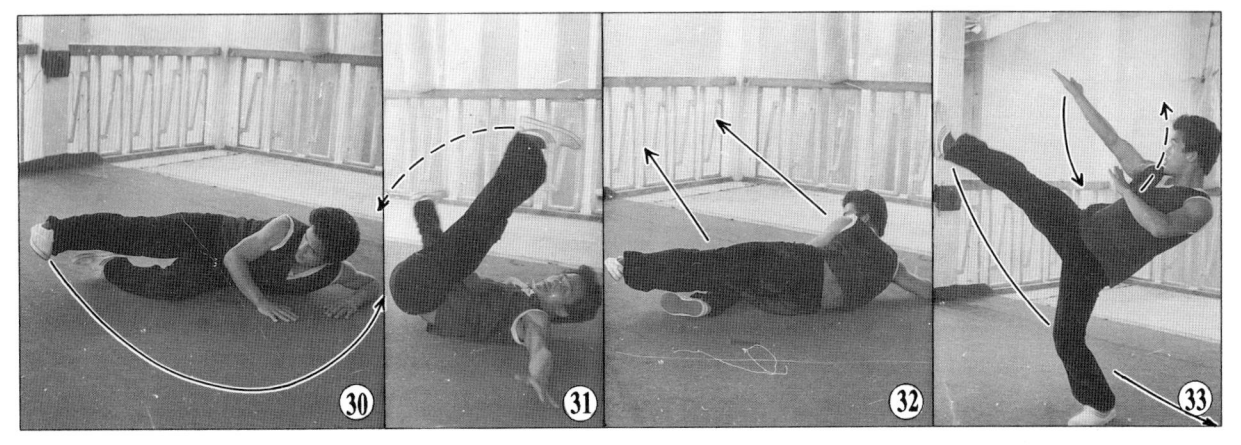

rear. Turn the head to look in the direction of the left foot. **(Fig. 29)**

17. Pierce with Right Leg

Bend the left leg and place it under the body. Sway the torso to the left side to form a left lying position, with both hands and the left forearm placed on the ground to support the torso. Then, the right leg pierces horizontally to the right, with its toes turned in and force concentrated on the outer edge of the foot. Fix your eyes on the right foot. **(Fig. 30)**

18. Left Butterfly Legs

1) Lie on your back while the right leg sweeps horizontally clockwise, passing before the face, then to the right. The left leg follows to sweep in a horizontal circle. Prop the buttocks and the waist up and keep the legs naturally apart while they are twisting in the air. **(Fig. 31)**

2) Without any pause, turn the body to a right lying position with both hands placed on the ground to support the torso, keeping the arms bent. At the same time, bend the right leg with its outer side touching the ground, and stretch the left leg above the right one with its toes resting on the ground. Turn the head to look to the upper left. **(Fig. 32)**

19. Pierce with Right Leg

As you stand up on the slightly bent left leg, with the torso leaning backward, the right leg pierces to the front, keeping the ankle straight. Force is concentrated on the toes of the foot. Simultaneously, stretch the right hand to the upper front, and hold the left hand crosswise in front of the chest with the arm bent. Fix your eyes on the fingers of the right hand. **(Fig. 33)**

20. Back Arc Kick

1) As the right foot lowers and lands behind, the right palm hacks down and swings backward. Meanwhile, the left hand blocks a blow to the upper left. Turn the torso to the right and fix your eyes on the right palm. **(Fig. 34)**

2) Without any pause, the right leg bends at the knee, and the left foot takes a step backward with the ball placed on the ground to form a cross-legged stance. At the same time, both arms swings upward and inward until they cross in front of the chest. **(Fig. 35)**

3) Without any pause, set the sole of the left foot firmly on the ground and shift

your weight onto the left leg. As the torso leans forward, the right leg swings in an arc backward and upward. Meanwhile, lower both arms and separate them. The right hand then swings backward and upward, while the left hand tilts forward and upward. Fix your eyes on the right foot. (**Fig. 36**)

21. Side Fall

The body leans to the right and falls down with the left leg fully bent at the knee; while the right foot drops and then slides on the ground to the left. Simultaneously, the right arm swings downward, passing before the abdomen, then upward and finally to the right, drawing a complete vertical circle before it is placed on the ground to support the torso. The left hand drops to support the torso in front of the chest in the meantime. (**Fig. 37**)

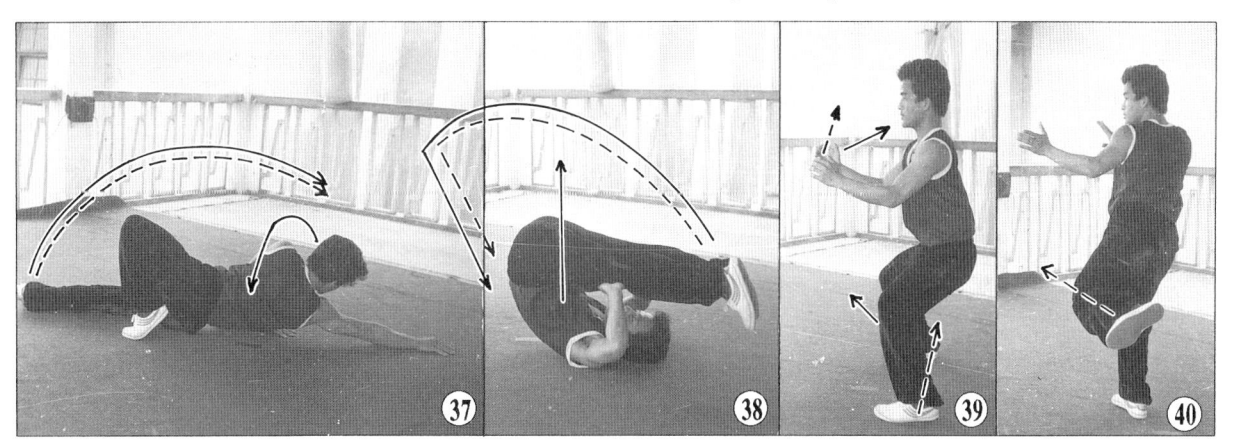

22. Carp Up-Jumping

1) Lie on your back with both legs stretched together, keeping the ankle straightened. Then, bend the hips, swinging both legs upward and folding them up close to the torso. Simultaneously, place both hands separately on the thighs with the arms bent. (**Fig. 38**)

2) Without any pause, exert the strength of the muscles on your back and waist to swing both legs upward, with both hands pushing the thighs forcefully so as to quicken the legs' motion. As the torso comes up with the hips straightened, both legs continue to press down swiftly with

35

knees slightly bent, to land on the balls of the feet. The movement ends when you stand up with both arms naturally bent and held in front of the body to keep balance. **(Fig. 39)**

23. Front Tread and Side Kick

1) As the right foot takes a step to the left front, the left foot rises behind with the knee slightly bent. At the same time, the left hand stretches a little forward; while the right hand draws a little back to the front of the chest. Keep both arms naturally bent. **(Fig. 40)**

2) Without any pause, the left foot treads with its heel towards the lower front; while both hands swings slightly to the right. **(Fig. 41)**

3) As the torso turns to the right with the toes of the right foot turned out, the left leg continues to kick with the outer edge of the foot towards the lower left. At the same time,, the left hand presses to the lower left; while the right hand blocks a blow to the upper right. **(Fig. 42)**

24. Front Sweep

Squat down on the ball of the left foot and stretch the right leg sideways with the toes turned in. Turn the torso quickly to the left and place both hands on the ground so that the right leg sweeps counterclockwise in a semicircle, with the sole close to the ground. **(Fig. 43)**

25. Right and Left Single Bat Stances

1) Bend the right leg at the knee and shift the weight onto the right leg, with the inner side of the left lower leg and foot placed on the ground to form a right single bat stance. At the same time, the right hand blocks a blow to the upper right with the hollow of the hand facing obliquely upward; while the left hand presses to the lower left with the hollow of the hand facing obliquely outward. Look to the lower left. **(Fig. 44)**

2) Bend the left leg at the knee and shift the weight onto the left leg, with the inner side of the right lower leg and foot placed on the ground to form a left single bat stance. At the same time, the left hand blocks a blow to the upper left; while the

right hand presses to the lower right. Look to the lower right. (**Fig. 45**)

26. Back Arc Kick with Leg Bent

As the torso turns to the left to stand on the slightly bent left leg, the right leg swings backward and upward with the knee bent and the ankle straightened. The right hand slaps the outer side of the right foot behind. Turn the head to the right and fix your eyes on the right palm. (**Fig. 46**)

27. Jumping Front Kick to Double Bat Stance

As the right foot lands in front, the left leg swings upward. When the body rises in the air with a powerful jump, the right leg kicks forward and upward. The right hand then slaps the instep of the right foot in front of the face; while the left hand stretches out to the upper left. When dropping, bend both legs with the thighs together and heels apart to land on the ground, forming a double bat stance, with both arms bent and held in front of the chest. Look forward. (**Fig. 47**)

28. Backward Roll

Fall on your back and roll backward with both legs and arms naturally bent. (**Fig. 48**)

29. Left Single Bat Stance

After you turn over, squat down on the left leg, with the inner side of the right lower leg and foot placed on the ground to form a left single bat stance. The left hand blocks a blow to the upper left with the arm bent and the hollow of the palm facing obliquely upward; while the right hand presses to the lower right with the hollow of the palm facing obliquely outward. Look to the lower right. (**Fig. 49**)

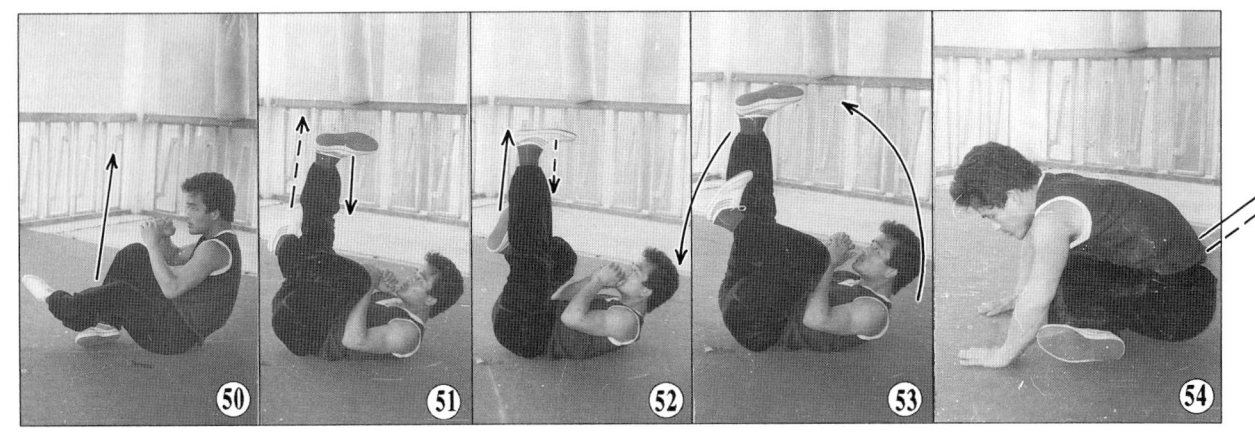

30. Rascally Dog Kicks with Its Heel Three Times

1) Turn the body about 180 degrees to the right with the toes of the left foot turned in, and then sit down on the ground. Hold both fists in front of the chest with the arms naturally bent. (**Fig. 50**)

2) Lie on your back. Bend both legs and draw the knees close to the torso. The right leg then kicks forcefully upward with its heel. (**Fig. 51**)

3) Without any pause, as the right leg drops with its knee bent, the left leg kicks forcefully upward with its heel. (**Fig. 52**)

4) Without any pause, as the left leg drops with its knee bent, the right leg again kicks forcefully upward with its heel. (**Fig. 53**)

31. Kick Backward with Both Legs

1) The body rolls slightly forward with legs crossed and hands placed on the ground to sit up. Look downward. (**Fig. 54**)

2) With the arms pushing the ground to prop the body up, both legs kick to the upper rear, keeping the ankles straight and the feet slightly apart. (**Fig. 55**)

3) Lower the feet and bend the legs so as to crouch on the balls of the feet, with both palms still on the ground to support the torso (there is a mistake in the figure,

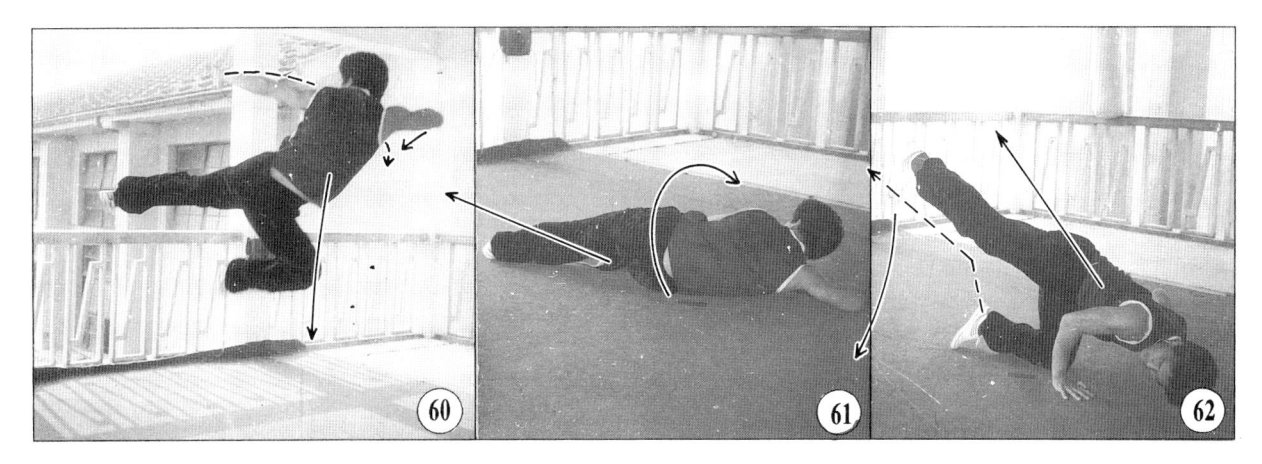

and you should make palms instead of fists). Look straight ahead. (**Fig. 56**)

32. Side Drop

1) The right foot takes a step forward with its toes turned out. Shift the weight forward with the heel of the left foot raised. As the right hand swings forward with the hollow of the palm facing upward, the left hand comes up and then presses on the crook of the right arm with the hollow of the palm facing downward. (**Fig. 97**)

2) Without any pause, the left leg swings upward with the knee bent. (**Fig. 58**)

3) Continuing from the preceding movement, straighten the right leg quickly and forcefully to jump up. (**Fig. 59**)

4) As the body rises in the air, turn the torso to the right and raise the right leg with the knee bent. The left leg kicks horizontally sideways with the toes turned in and force concentrated on the outer edge of the foot. At the same time, the right hand draws back to the front of the chest; while the left palm pushes horizontally sideways, force concentrated on the little-finger side of the hand. (**Fig. 60**)

5) The body leans to the right and then drops down. While landing, keep the right leg bent and the left leg stretched. The outer side of the right leg, the sole of the left foot, the right forearm and both the palms touch the ground at the same time. (**Fig. 61**)

33. Tiger Tail Leg

Turn the body to the right so as to kneel down on the left knee. Place both hands on the ground with the arms bent to support the torso. Meanwhile, the right leg kicks with its heel to the upper rear. Turn the head to the right and look in the direction of the right foot. (**Fig. 62**)

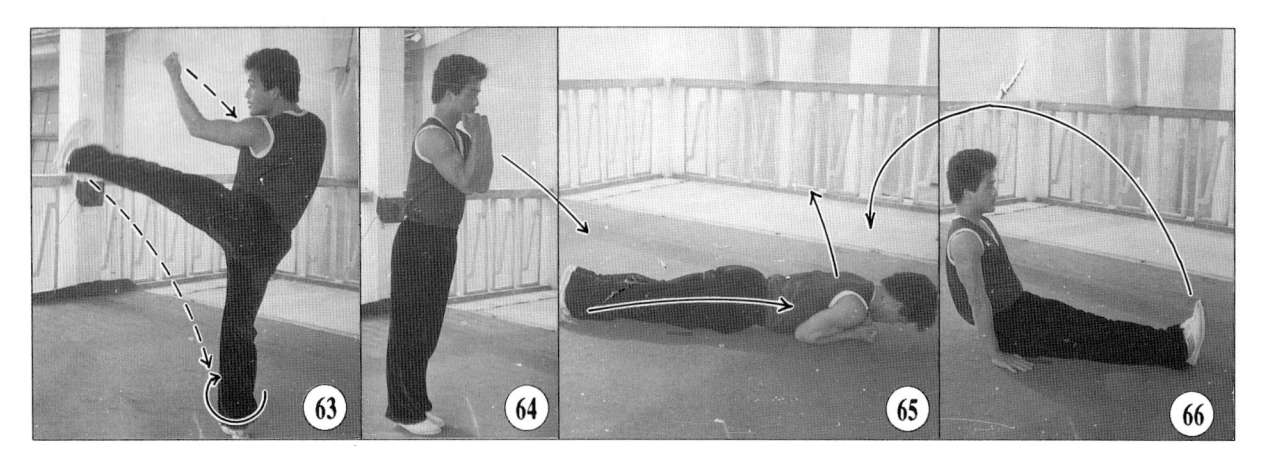

34. Kick with Left Leg

With the right foot landing on the ground, the torso turns to the left to stand up on the right leg. The left leg then kicks sideways with its heel. At the same time, clench both fists. The left fist swings sideways up to head level; while the right fist pauses in front of the chest. Keep both arms bent. Look to the left side. **(Fig. 63)**

35. Straight Body Fall

1) Lower the left foot. Turn the body to the right to stand upright with the feet together. Hold both fists in front of the shoulder with the arms bent and the hollows of the fists facing the torso. Look straight ahead. **(Fig. 64)**

2) Lean forward and fall down, keeping the body straight as a stone tablet, landing with the outer sides of the forearms to support the body. **(Fig. 65)**

3) Place both hands on the ground and straighten the arms to prop the body up. With the hips bent, both legs then penetrate forward through the space between the arms, so as to sit up with legs straight and feet hooked. **(Fig. 66)**

36. Left Single Bat Stance

Lie on your back and swing legs upward to roll backward. After you turn over, squat on the left leg with the inner side of the right lower leg and foot placed on the ground to form a left single bat stance. At the same time, the left hand blocks a blow to the upper left with the arm bent; while the right hand presses to the lower right. Look to the right front. (**Fig. 67**)

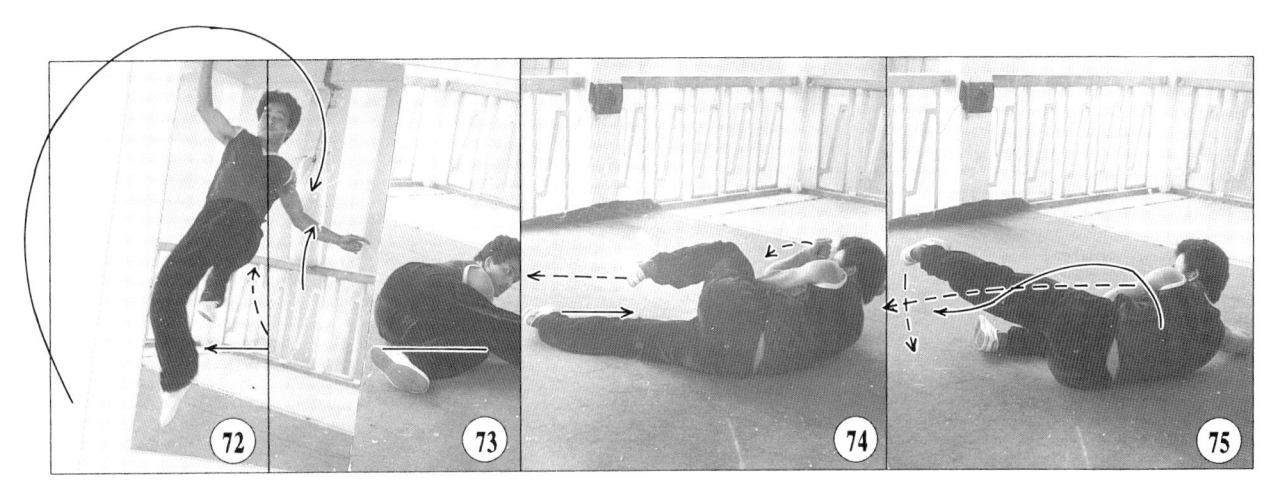

37. Kick with Right Leg

Stand up on the slightly bent left leg. The right leg then kicks to the lower front with the torso leaning backward and turning slightly to the right. Meanwhile, the right hand swings in a vertical arc inward and upward, then makes a grab to the right front. Simultaneously, the left hand drops upon the right forearm. Fix your eyes on the right foot. (**Fig. 68**)

38. Cross-legged Drop

1) The right foot takes a step backward. As the torso turns to the right, bend the right leg at the knee and straighten the left leg. At the same time, the left hand presses down to the front of the abdomen; while the right hand clenches into a fist and withdraws to the right side of the waist. (**Fig. 69**)

2) Turn the torso to the left while the left foot draws a small circle inward before stepping to the front again. The left hand swings upward and makes a grab to the front in the meantime. (**Fig. 70**)

3) Continuing from the preceding movement, the right foot takes a step forward with its toes turned in and those of the left foot out. Following the body turn, the right fist swings up from the back, and then forward until it reaches out to the right side at shoulder level; while the left hand clenches into a fist and withdraws to the front of the chest. Fix your eyes on the right fist. (**Fig. 71**)

4) Without any pause, the left arm swings downward, passing before the abdomen, then to the left. At the same time, swing the left leg sideways up with the knee bent, and straighten the right leg quickly and forcefully to jump up into the air. Turn the body about 270 degrees to the left through the jump. (**Fig. 72**)

5) The body continues to turn about 90 degrees to the left and leans to the left side; while the right leg swings upward and around until it presses down to the right side. The body then drops down with both legs crossed like a pair of scissors. While

41

landing, the outer side of the left leg and both the forearms touch the ground in the meantime, keeping the arms bent. Look to the right. (**Fig. 73**)

39. Hook and Kick with Legs

1) Turn the torso to the left and lie on the right side of the body. Place the right arm on the ground to support the torso, with the left fist held in front of the face to protect the head. At the same time, the right leg pierces along the ground to the left; while the left leg pulls up with the knee bent and the foot hooked. (**Fig. 74**)

2) As the left hand is also placed on the ground too to maintain a steady lying position, the left leg kicks forcefully with its heel to the left. Simultaneously, the right leg pulls up with the knee bent and the foot hooked. (**Fig. 75**)

40. Penetrate Ahead and Kick with Both Legs

1) The left foot lands on the ground with the knee bent. Both hands push the ground so that the torso sways to the left side. The body then penetrates ahead along the ground, as if through the space under the opponent's crotch, with the left arm leading the penetration and the right hand held overhead. Stretch the right leg and keep the left leg bent when the body falls on the ground. (**Fig. 76**)

2) Turn the torso to the right so as to lie on your back, with the head inclined a little forward. Place the arms on both sides on the ground. Bend both legs and draw the knees up close to the torso. (**Fig. 77**)

3) Without any pause, both legs kick obliquely upward with the feet a little apart. Fix your eyes on the feet. (**Fig. 78**)

41. Carp Up-jumping

Bend the hips and swing the legs towards the head, with both hands separately placed on the thighs. Then, swing both legs upward with both hands pushing the thighs forcefully so as to quicken the legs' motion. As the torso comes up with the hips straightened, both legs continue to press down swiftly with the knees slightly bent, to land with the feet a step-width apart to form a horse-riding step. Keep both arms naturally bent and hold them in front of the torso. (**Fig. 79**)

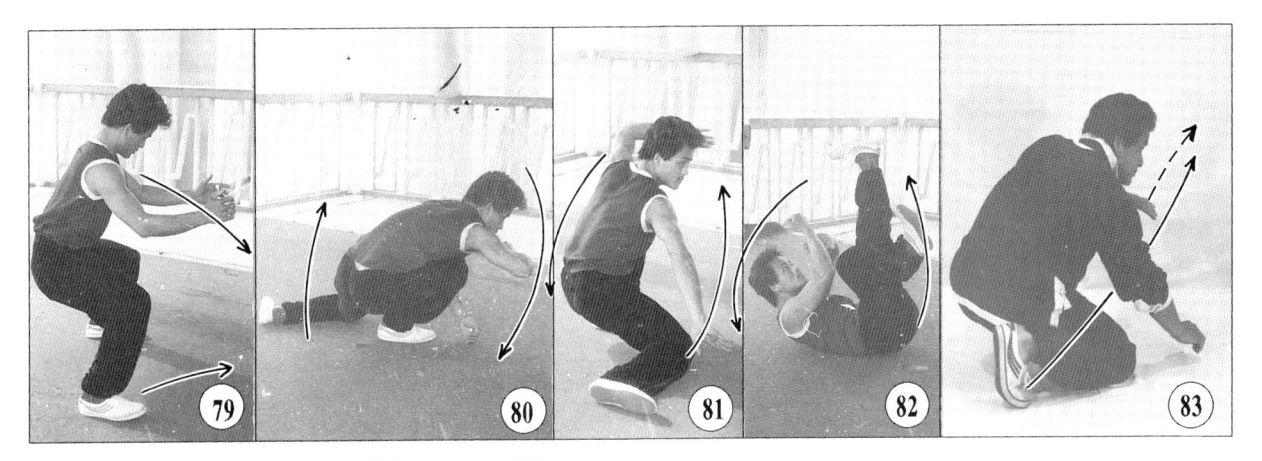

42. Shoulder Roll

Bow the torso down while the right foot moves a step forward. Then, perform a shoulder roll. (**Fig. 80**)

43. Left Single Bat Stance

On completing the shoulder roll, squat down on the left leg with the inner side of the right lower leg and foot placed on the ground to form a left single bat stance. (**Fig. 81**)

44. Backward Roll

1) Fall on your back and roll backward. (**Fig. 82**)

2) After you turn over, squat down on the left leg with the inner side of the right lower leg and foot placed on the ground to form a left single bat stance. With the arms straight, both hands remain on the ground to prop the torso up. (**Fig. 83**)

45. Swing Right Leg Inward

Stand up on the slightly bent left leg. While the knee straightened, the right leg then swings in a fan-shaped curve, first sideways up, then inward. Simultaneously, the left hand slaps the sole of the right foot in front of the torso; while the right hand clenches into a fist and withdraws to the right side of the waist. (**Fig. 84**)

46. Hack with Right in Bow Step

Without any pause, the right foot drops and lands behind. Bend the left leg at the knee and straighten the right leg to form a left bow step. At the same time, with the arm straightened, the right fist swings up from the back, then froward, and finally hacks down to the lower front; while the left palm withdraws to the front of the chest with the arm bent. (**Fig. 85**)

47. Closing Form

1) Bend the right leg and shift your weight backward. Draw the left foot next to the right one and rest its toes on the ground to form a left T-step. Meanwhile, withdraw the right fist to the right side of the waist, with the left palm lowered against the right fist. (**Fig. 86**)

2) After the left foot takes a side step, the right foot advances with its toes resting on the ground to form a right empty step. Meanwhile, the right fist and the left palm together push straight ahead. (**Fig. 87**)

3) Draw the right foot back and move it sideways to form a horse-riding step. Meanwhile, open the right fist and turn the hollows of the hands up. Both palms then separate sideways with the arms slightly bent. **(Fig. 88)**

4) Without any pause, draw both hands to the sides of the waist. Then, turn the hollows of the hands down and push both hands forward, with the fingers pointing obliquely inward. Force is concentrated on the little-finger side of the hands. **(Fig. 89)**

5) Bring the left foot next to the right one. Stand upright with both legs straightened. Both arms hang down naturally to the sides of the body. Look horizontally forward. **(Fig. 90)**

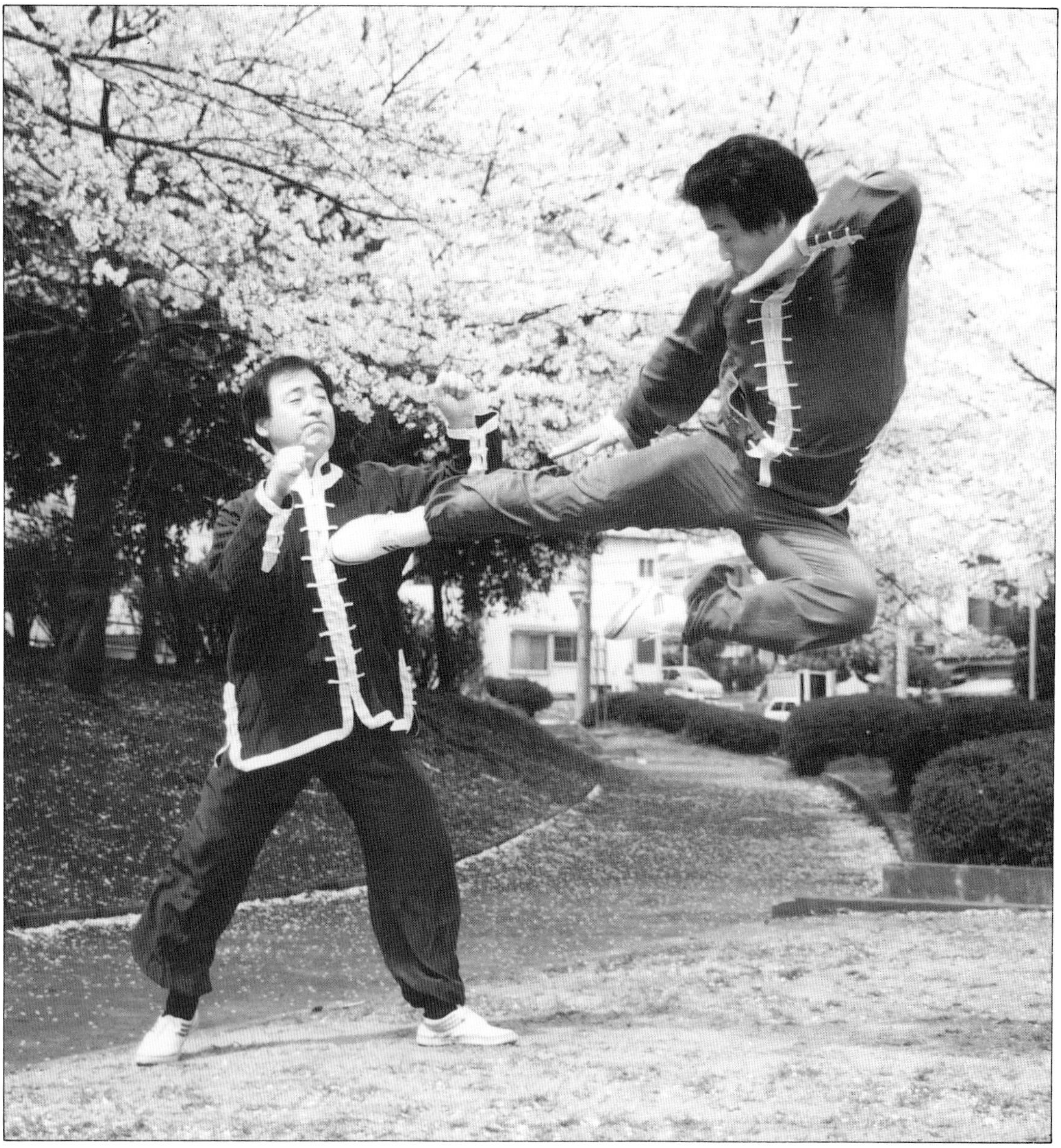

Chapter Four: The Paired Practice

Preparatory Form
(1)
Both **A** (dressed in black) and **B** (dressed in white) stand upright with feet together, confronting each other. The distance between the two is about 3 meters.

Fist-holding Salute
(2)
A and **B**: Bend the left leg at the knee and move the right foot forward with the toes resting on the ground to form a right empty step. Meanwhile, the right hand clenches into a fist. Both the right fist and the left palm then push forward from beside the waist, with the left palm adhering to the right fist. Fix your eyes on opponent.

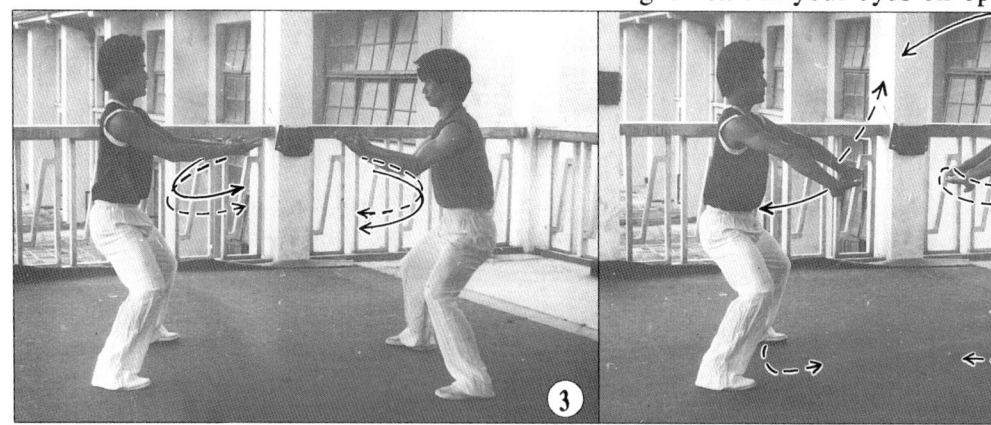

Separate Palms Sideways in Horse-riding Step
(3)
A and **B**: Draw the right foot back and move it sideways to form a horse-riding step, distributing the weight evenly on both legs. Meanwhile, open the right fist and turn the hollows of both hands up. Both palms then separate sideways with the arms naturally bent.

Cut Forward with Both Palms in Horse-riding Step
(4)
A and **B**: Without any pause, draw both hands to the sides of the waist, then push them forward with the hollows of the palms turned down, the fingers pointing inward.

(5)

    B: After the right foot advances, the left foot takes another step forward to form a left bow step. At the same time, clench both hands into fists. The left fist draws back to the left side of the waist; while the right fist swings backward and upward, then smashes forward.

    A: The left foot takes a step forward to form a left semi-horse-riding step. At the same time, clench both hands into fists. The left fist swings to the upper front to block B's blow; while the right fist withdraws to the right side of the waist.

(6)

    B: Shift the weight onto the left leg. Raise the right leg with the knee bent. The right foot then kicks quickly forward with the ankle straightened. Meanwhile, hold both fists in front of the chest with the arms bent.

    A: The left foot retreats to the back to form a right semi-horse-riding step. At the same time, open both fists. The right hand comes forward to slap **B**'s right foot down; while the left hand withdraws to the front of the right shoulder.

(7)

    A: Turn the torso to the right and shift the weight onto the right leg. The left leg then swings forward and to the right to hook **B**'s leg. Meanwhile, hold the right hand in front of the chest, with the left arm naturally hanging down.

    B: The right foot drops and lands behind. As the weight is shifted backward onto the right leg, raise the left leg with the knee bent.

(8)

A: When the hooking comes to nothing, the torso turns to the right. The left leg then changes to kick **B** on the inner side of the right knee.

(9)

B: Following **A**'s kicking force, **B** falls down, forming a right lying stance on the ground.

A: The left foot lands on the ground tp form a left semi-horse-riding step.

(10)

A: Shift the weight onto the left leg. The right leg then comes ahead to tread on **B**'s left leg.

B: Turn the torso to the left to form a left lying stance. With the left leg butting against **A**'s right ankle, the right leg hooks **A** by the hollow of the right knee in order to trip him.

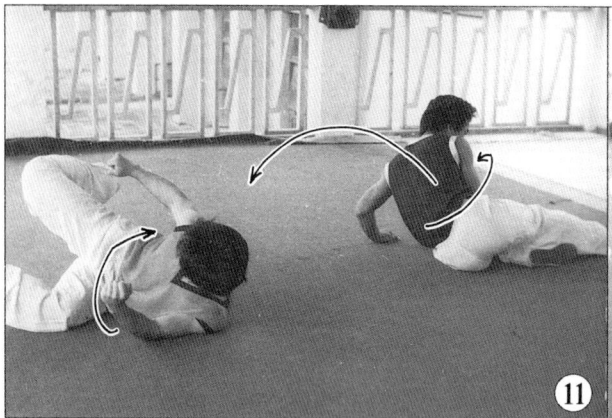

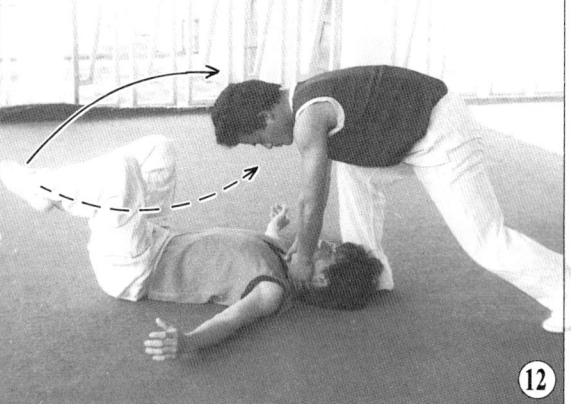

(11)

A: Following **B**'s tripping force, **A** bows down and goes on rolling forward with the right shoulder and the back of the torso touching the ground in succession.

(12)

B: Lie on the back.

A: Stand up quickly and turn round to seize **B** by the throat.

(13)

B: While gripping **A**'s forearms with the hands and pushing them upward, swing both legs upward to lock **A** by the neck from both sides.

(14)

B: Hold both legs firmly together and swing them forward and downward with great strength in order to throw **A** on the ground.

A: Following **B**'s force, the body bows down and rolls forward.

(15)

A: Complete the following roll with a right single bat stance.

B: Swing both legs upwards so as to perform a "carp up-jumping".

(16)

A: The torso turns to the left to form a left semi-horse-riding step. Hold both fists in front of the chest with the arms bent, the left fist being further ahead.

B: Stand up with the feet apart and the legs slightly bent. Hold both fists in front of the chest with the arms bent, the right fist being further ahead.

51

(17)
A: As the right foot takes a step forward to form a right semi-horse-riding step, the right fist thrusts straight ahead with the eye of the fist facing upward. Meanwhile, open the left fist and withdraw the palm to the front of the right shoulder with the wrist dropped down and fingers pointing upward.
B: The right foot takes a step backward to form a left semi-horse-riding step. Simultaneously, the left fist opens and presses down to ward off A's right fist; while the right fist withdraws to the right side of the waist.

(18)
B: While turning A's right arm aside with the left hand, the right foot takes a step toward the back of A's front foot and then draws back to trip A. Simultaneously, the right fist swings from the side to the front to hook A by the neck.

(19)
A: At the very moment, A falls down with the right shoulder first touching the ground and then penetrates through the space under B's crotch, the head leading the penetration. After that, A lies on the back with legs bent and drawn up, clutching B's ankles with the hands and pressing the legs against B's knees from inside to prevent B from sitting down.

(20)
A: Without any pause, A raises the right foot to kick B on the buttocks so as to force him to fall forward. Release the hold when B loses his balance.

(21)

B: While the body falls down, **B** turns to the right to form a left lying stance.

A: Stand up quickly. Then, step forward and raise the right foot to tread on **B**'s right lower leg.

(22)

B: Before **A** bears down with all his weight on **B**'s right leg, B seizes **A**'s right foot with the right hand and turns it out forcefully. **B**'s right foot then bumps against the hollow of **A**'s right knee and kicks out.

(23)

B: Stand up quickly and step forward with the left leg to form a left bow step. Simultaneously, the right fist swings up from the back, then smashes forward and downward; while the left fist withdraws to the left side of the waist.

A: Being kicked at, **A** bows down and rolls forward with the right shoulder and the back of the torso touching the ground in succession. After that, **A** squats on the left leg with the inner side of the right lower leg and foot placed on the ground to form a left single bat stance. The right fist swings up to block **B**'s blow in the meantime.

(24)

B: As the torso turns to the left with the weight shifted onto the left leg, **B** raises the right foot to tread on **A**'s right flank.

A: The right fist swings downward and backward to parry **B**'s right leg.

53

(25)

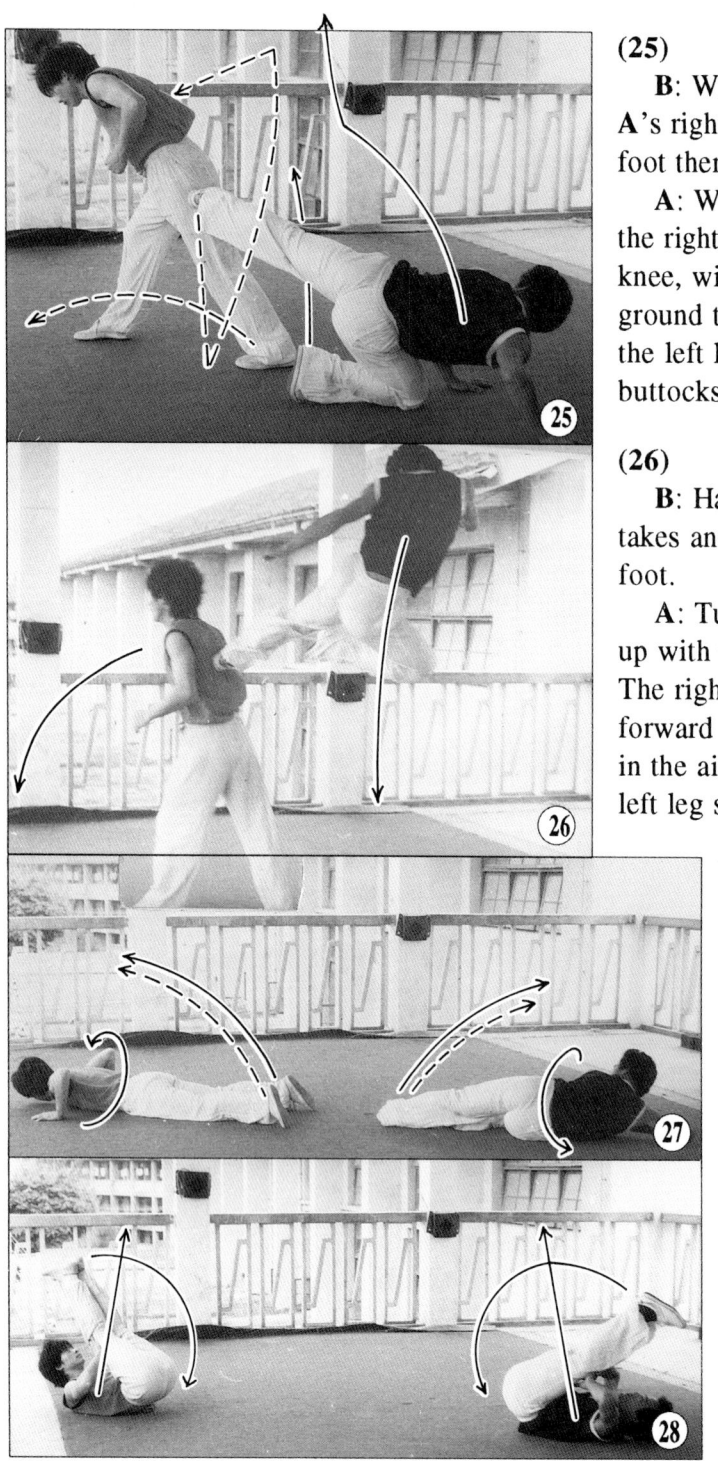

B: When the right leg is turned aside by **A**'s right arm, **B** turns to the left. The right foot then lands in front.

A: Without any pause, turn the torso to the right so as to kneel down on the right knee, with both hands placed on the ground to support the body. Meanwhile, the left leg kicks backward towards **B**'s buttocks.

(26)

B: Having been hit on the buttocks, **B** takes another step forward with the left foot.

A: Turn the torso to the left and stand up with the left foot placed on the ground. The right foot immediately takes a step forward to jump up. While the body rises in the air, bend the right leg and stretch the left leg sideways to kick **B** on the back.

(27)

B: Having been hit on the back, the body falls forward onto the ground.

A: The body leans to the right and drops down. While landing, the outer side of the right leg, the sole of the left foot, the right forearm and both the hands touch the ground at the same time.

(28)

A and **B**: Turn the body to lie on the back. Then, swing legs upward to start a "carp up-jumping".

(29)

A and B: After the "carp up-jumping", stand up with the legs slightly bent and feet a step apart.

(30)

B: As the right foot takes a step forward, the right fist thrusts straight ahead. The left fist withdraws to the left side of the waist in the meantime.

A: As the right foot takes a step forward, the right hand swings forward to make a grab at B's right wrist. The left fist withdraws to the left side of the waist in the meantime.

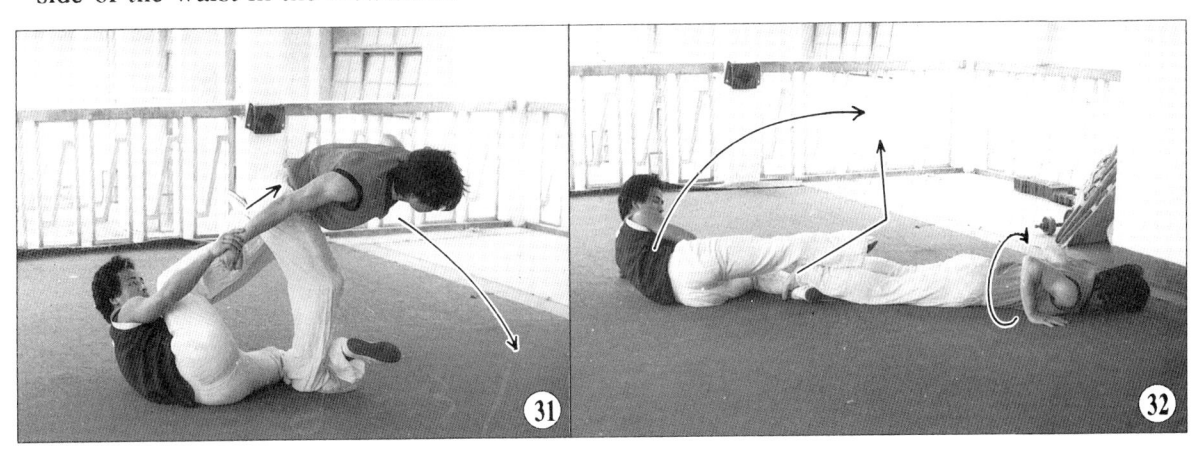

(31)

A: Without any pause, the left foot advances towards the back of B's front foot. Then, A lies down on the ground, twisting B's right arm behind his back. Meanwhile, raise the right foot to bump against B's buttocks.

(32)

A: Loosen the grip when the right leg kicks out.

B: Following the kicking force, B falls forward onto the ground.

(33)

A: Stand up quickly and pounce forward on **B**.

B: Turn the body to lie on the back, with the left leg bent. Raise the right foot to kick upward on **A**'s belly.

(34)

A: After having been forced to perform a forward roll, **A** lies on the back and swings the legs respectively to start a "right butterfly legs"

B: Swing both legs respectively to start a "right butterfly legs".

(35)

A and **B**: Squat on the right leg and place the inner side of the left lower leg and foot on the ground to form a right single bat stance, with the left side of the body towards the opponent.

(36)

B: Shift the weight onto the fully bent left leg. Turn the torso quickly to the left with both hands placed on the ground. Meanwhile, the right leg stretches sideways and sweeps counter-clockwise with the toes turned in and the sole close to the ground.

A: With a powerful jump, the body rises high into the air.

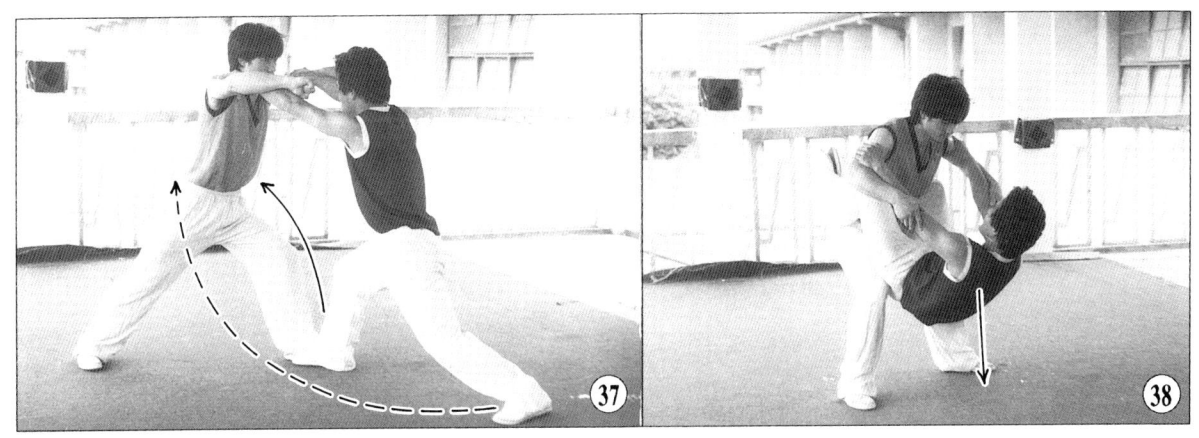

(37)

B: The body continues to turn round, making the right foot sweep in a complete circle. Then, stand up to form a left bow step. Both fists swing from both sides to the front in the meantime.

A: While the body drops down, bend the right leg at the knee and straighten the left leg to form a right bow step. Meanwhile, both arms swing upward and downward to block **B**'s strike.

(38)

A: While gripping **B**'s arms with the hands, **A** jumps up and hooks both legs around **B**'s waist.

(39)

A: While both hands slide down along **B**'s arms to grip **B** by the wrists, the torso drops onto the ground. Meanwhile, bend both legs to kick **B** on the belly.

(40)

B: As the body falls backward onto the ground, the right leg kicks upward with its heel.

A: Stand up quickly and pounce forward on **B**, with both hands seizing **B**'s right ankle firmly.

57

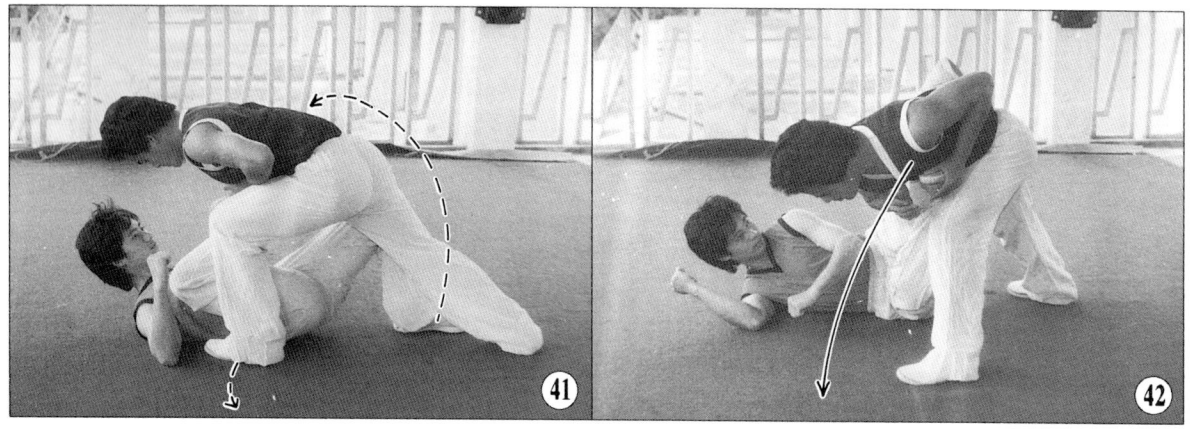

(41)

A: Bear down with all the weight and twist **B**'s foot outward.

(42)

B: When the right foot is wrenched out, turn the torso to the right and swing the left leg upward and inward to strike **A** on the right flank.

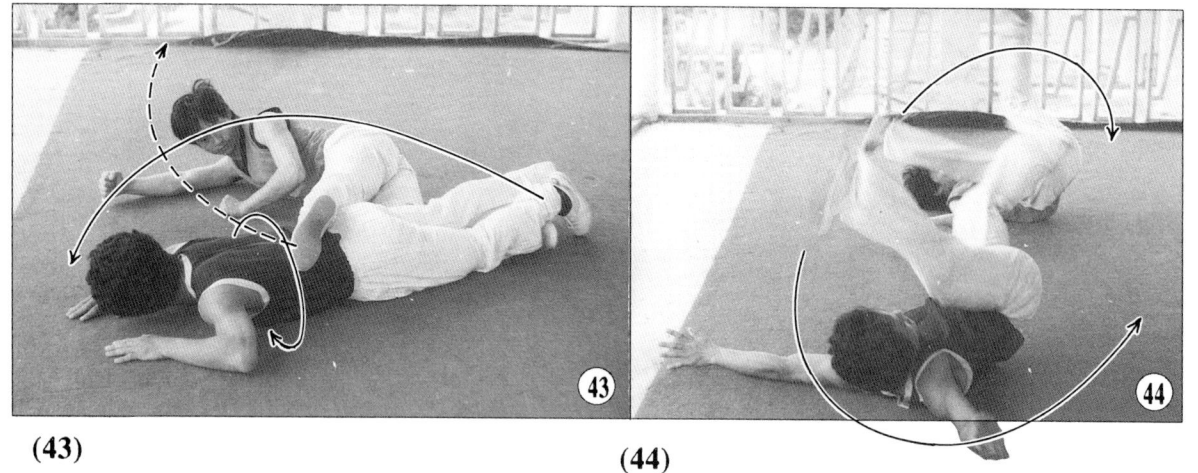

(43)

A: Having been hit by **B**'s left leg, **A** falls down in a prostrate position to the left front.

B: Lay the left leg upon **A**'s waist and press down.

(44)

A and **B**: Turn the body to lie on the back and swing the legs respectively to start a "right butterfly legs".

(45)

A and **B**: Continuing from the preceding movement, squat on the left leg and place the inner side of the right lower leg and foot on the ground to form a left single bat stance, with the right side of the body towards the opponent.

(46)

A and **B**: Turn the torso to the right and stand up to form a right semi-horse-riding step, the arms swing forward and upward to block the opponent's attack.

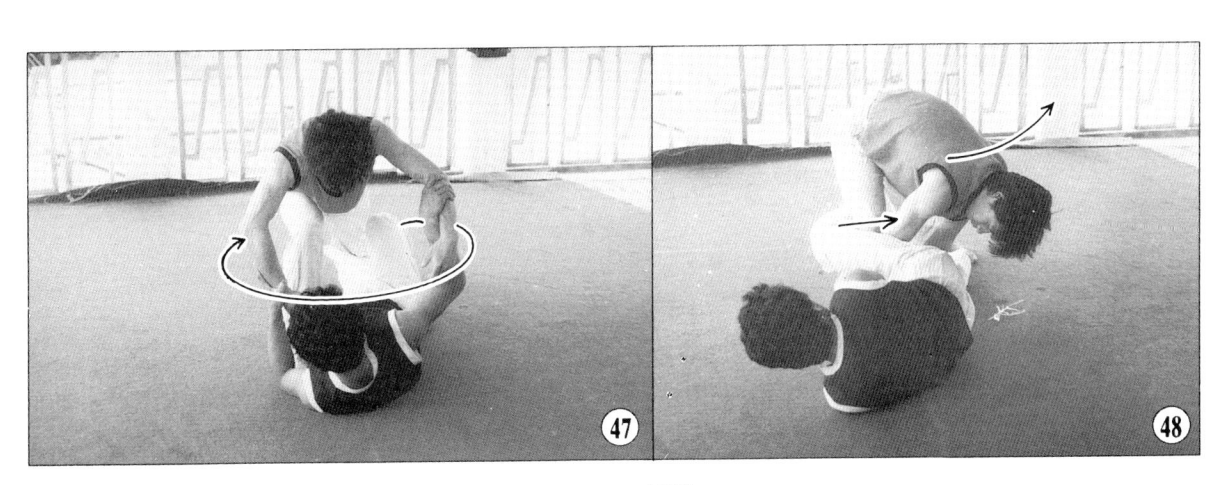

(47)

A: As the left foot slides ahead to bump against the inner side of **B**'s left foot, **A** takes the initiative to fall sideways down, with both hands gripping **B**'s forearms.

(48)

A: Without any pause, the right leg swings over to hook **B** by the hollow of his right knee.

59

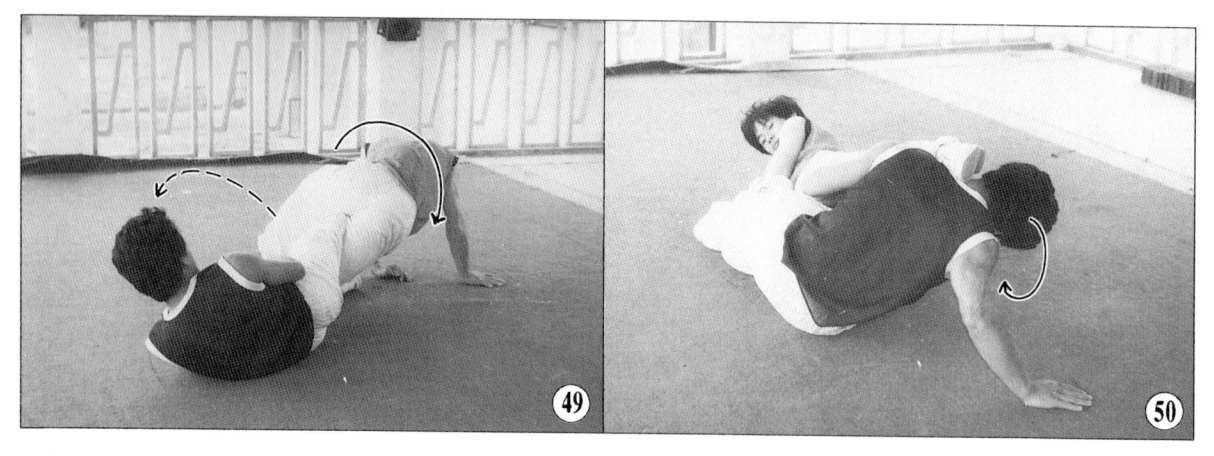

(49)

A: While the right leg extends to bump against **B**'s left knee, the body turns to the right with great strength in order to wrench **B** over. Both hands do not let go until **B** is forced to turn to the left and fall over.

(50)

B: While turning to the left so as to lie on the right side of the body, **B** swings the left leg horizontally backward to strike **A** on the head.

A: Sway the head aside and turn the torso to the right to dodge the blow of **B**'s left leg.

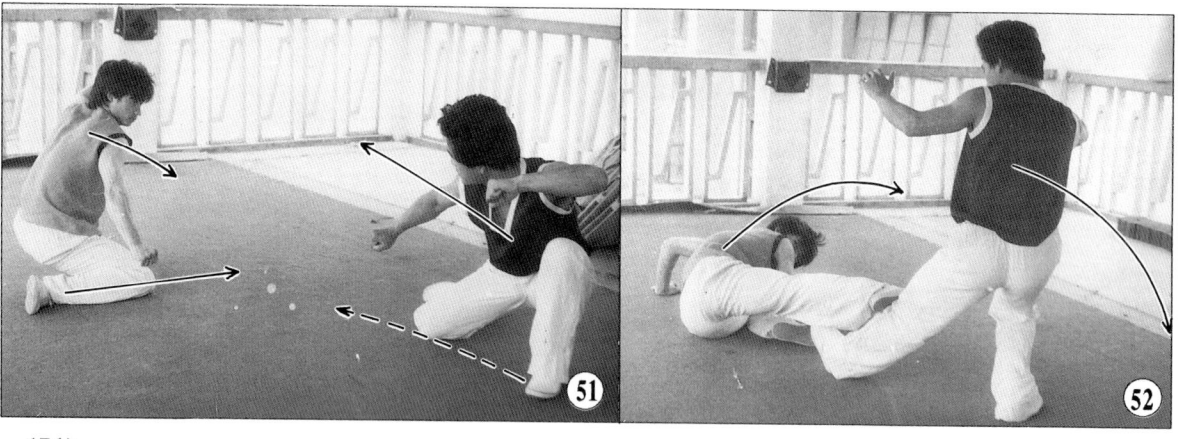

(51)

A and **B**: Lie on the back and then swing the legs respectively to start a "right butterfly legs". After that, squat on the left leg and place the inner side of the right lower leg and foot on the ground to from a left single bat stance, with the right side of the body towards the opponent.

(52)

B: As the torso leans to the left and lies prostrate with both hands placed on the ground to support the body, the right leg stretches out to kick **A** on the left knee.

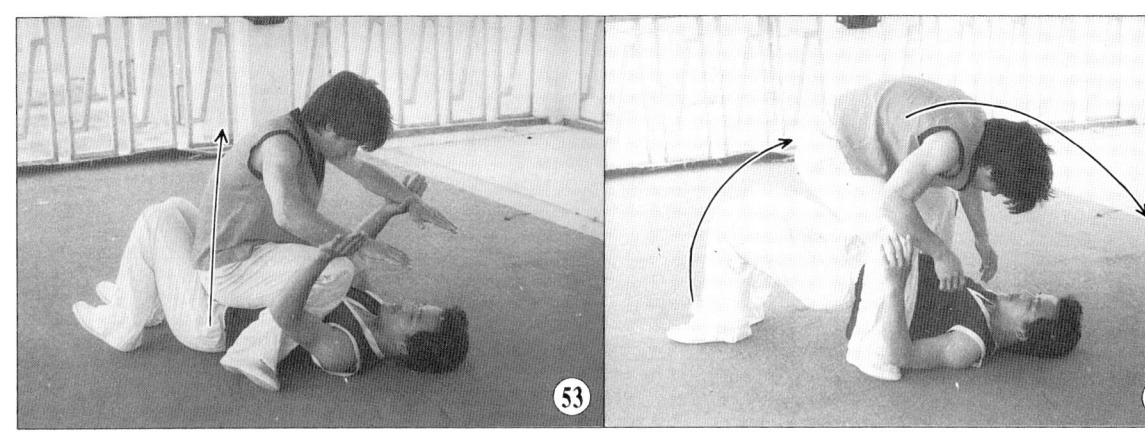

(53)
　A: The body falls backward onto the ground. When **B** pounces forward, grip **B**'s arms with both hands and push them up.
　B: Stand up quickly and then leap forward to sit down on **A**'s belly, with both hands pressing downward.

(54)
　A: Straighten the hips and thrust the belly up violently to toss **B**, forcing him to lean forward.

(55)
　A: Without any pause, **A** swings the right leg upward to bump against **B**'s buttocks.

　B: Having been hit by **A**'s right leg, **B** bows down and rolls forward with the right shoulder and the back of the torso touching the ground in succession.

(56)
　A: Stand up quickly with the back towards **B**.
　B: After the shoulder roll, **B** stands up swiftly and turns round to clasp **A** by the waist, with the right leg inserted between **A**'s legs.

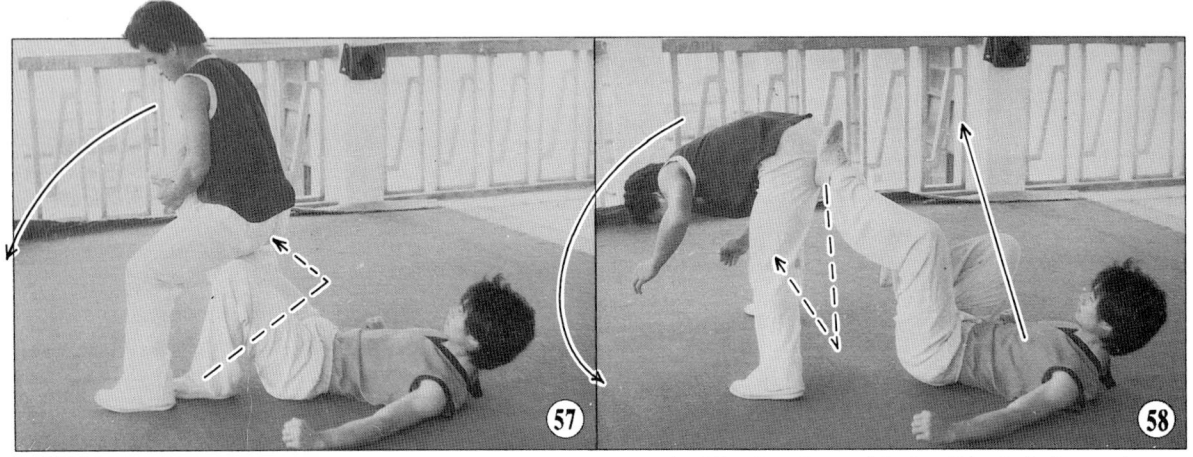

(57)

A: Sit down on **B**'s right thigh while the torso leans forward to catch hold of **B**'s right foot with both hands. Then, pull **B**'s right foot upward with great strength.

B: While losing balance, **B** is forced to fall backward onto the ground.

(58)

B: While lying on the back, **B** raises the left foot to kick **A** on the buttocks.

A: Having been hit by **B**'s left foot, **A** bows down and rolls forward.

(59)

B: Stand up quickly. The right foot then takes a step forward. Turn the torso to the right and shift the weight onto the right leg. Meanwhile, the left leg kicks to the upper left, with force concentrated on the outer edge of the foot. Hold both fists in front of the chest.

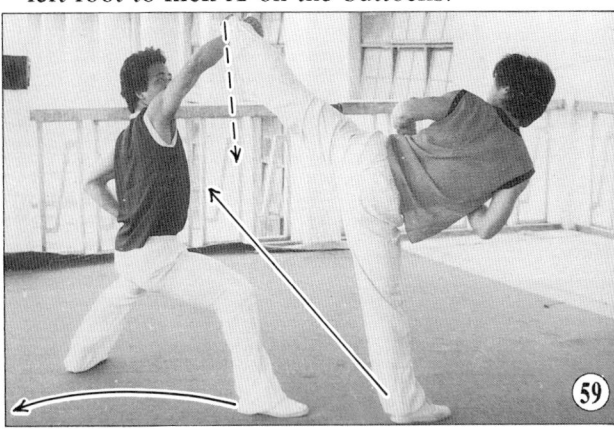

A: After the forward roll, the body comes up and turns round to the left, forming a right semi-horse-riding step. At the same time, the right fist swings forward and upward to block **B**'s left leg; while the left fist withdraws to the left side of the waist.

(60)

B: As the torso turns to the left, lower the left foot and shift the weight onto the left leg. The right leg then kicks straight ahead with its heel.

A: As the torso turns to the right, the right foot retreats to form a right bow step. Meanwhile, withdraw the right fist to the right side of the waist and swing the left arm forward and upward to hug **B**'s right leg.

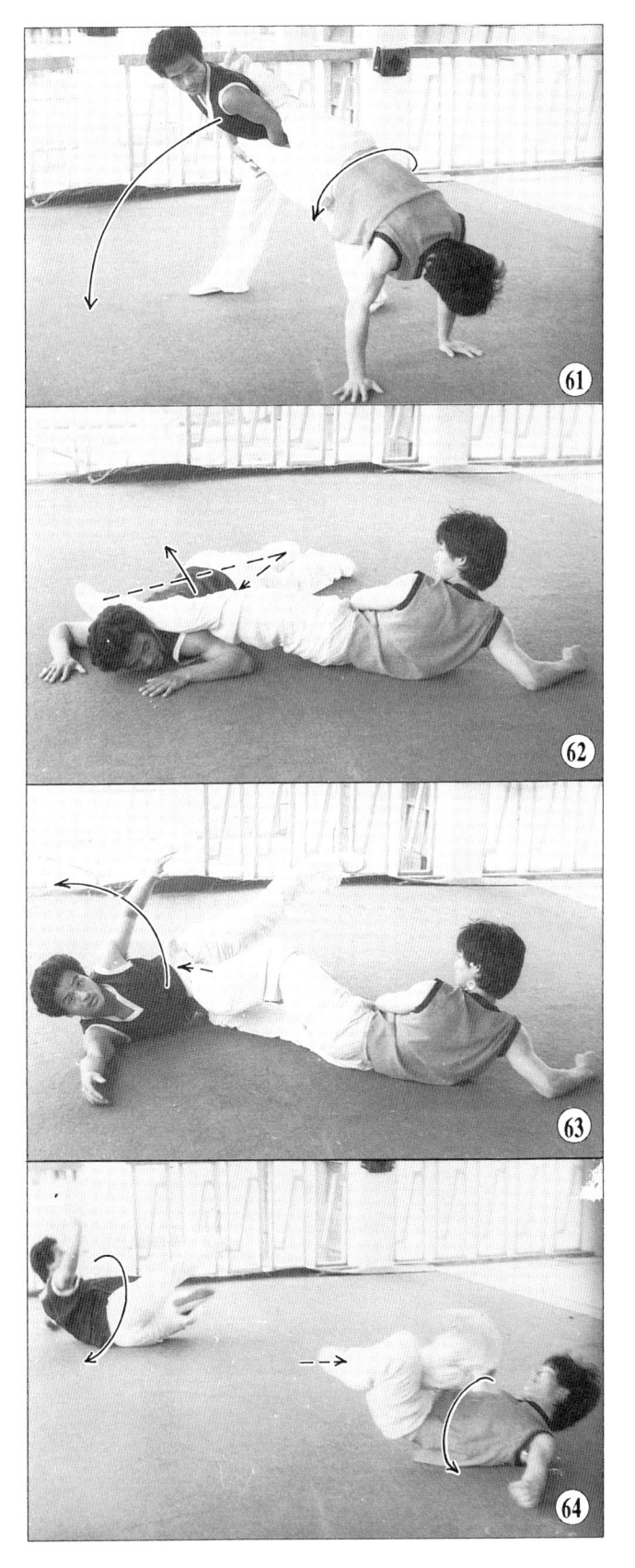

(61)

B: Without any pause, the body suddenly turns to the left, with both hands placed on the ground to support the torso. Simultaneously, the left leg swings backward and upward forcefully to strike **A** on the back.

(62)

A: Having been hit by **B**'s left leg, A falls in a prostrate position onto the ground.

B: The body continues to turn to the left to form a right lying stance, the left leg still pressing upon **A**'s shoulder.

(63)

B: Without any pause, raise the left leg to kick **A** on the waist with the heel.

A: Having been hit by **B**'s left leg, the body rolls longitudinally round to the left.

(64)

A and **B**: Lie on the back and begin to swing the legs respectively.

63

(65)

A and **B**: Perform a "right butterfly legs" respectively.

(66)

A and **B**: On completing the "right butterfly legs", squat on the left leg and place the inner side of the right lower leg and foot on the ground to form a left single bat stance, with the right side of the body towards the opponent.

(67)

A and **B**: Turn the torso to the right and stand up with both legs slightly bent and the toes of the right foot resting on the ground to form a right empty step. Meanwhile, hold the right fist and the left palm together in front of the torso, with the arms well rounded, as a salute to the opponent.

(68)

A and **B**: Draw the right foot back and move it sideways to form a horse-riding step. Meanwhile, open the right fist and turn the hollows of both hands up. Both palms then separate sideways with the arms naturally bent.

(69)

A and **B**: Draw both hands to the right of the waist, then push them forward with the hollows of the palms turned down, the fingers pointing inward.

(70)

A and **B**: Bring one foot next to the other to stand upright, facing each other, both arms hanging down naturally.

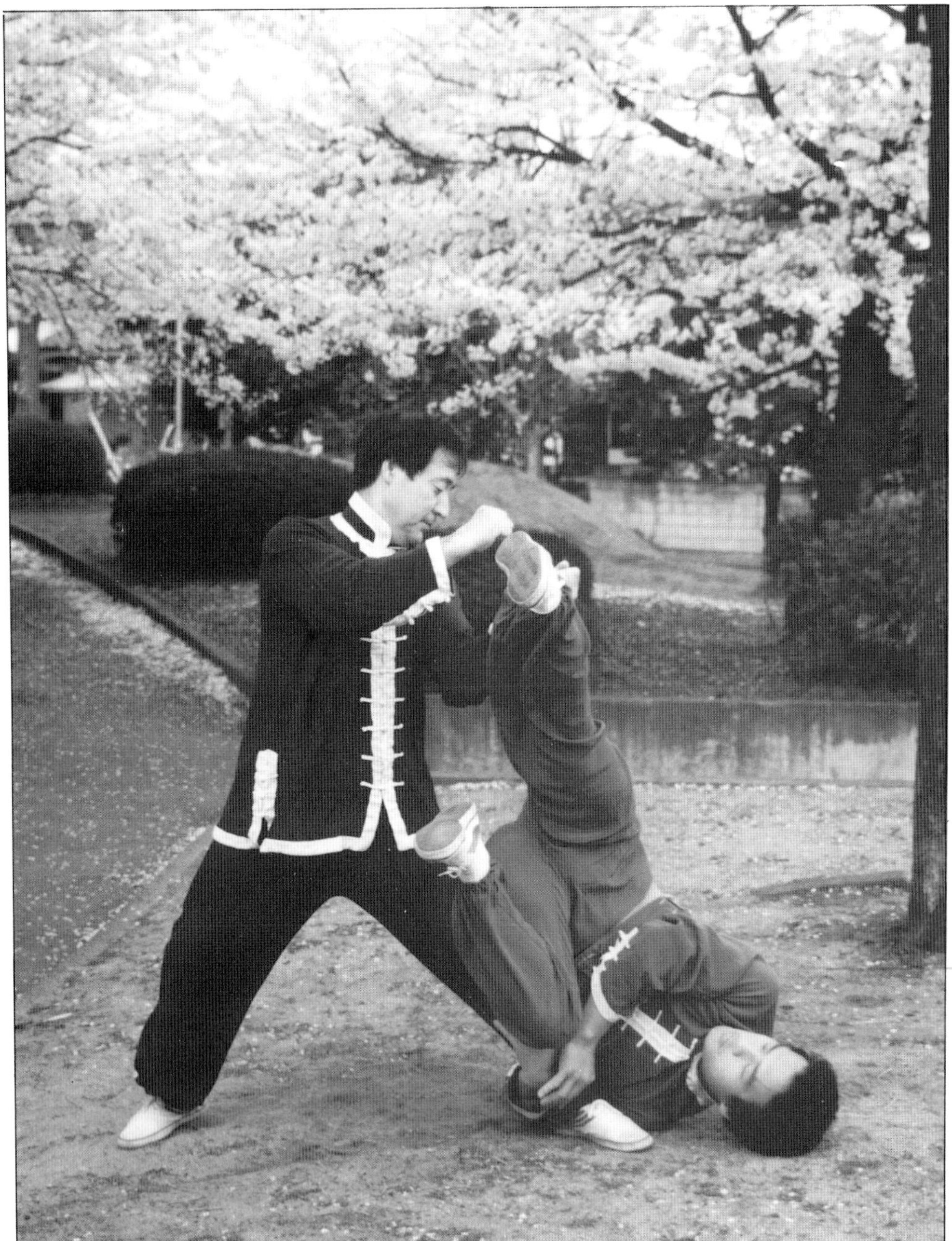

Chapter Five: The Essential Lower-level Skills for Actual Combat

1. The Carp Wags Its Tail

1) While **A** forms a left lying stance on the ground, **B** steps up raises the right foot to tread on **A**'s right knee.

2) **A** swings the right leg upward and outward to ward off **B**'s right leg.

3) While catching hold of **B**'s right foot with the right hand, **A** continues to swing the right leg outward until the foot presses against the back of **B**'s right thigh. The left leg stretches out to hook **B**'s left leg by the ankle in the meantime. Therefore, **B** is forced to turn round.

4) **A** does not release his hold until the right leg kicks forward.

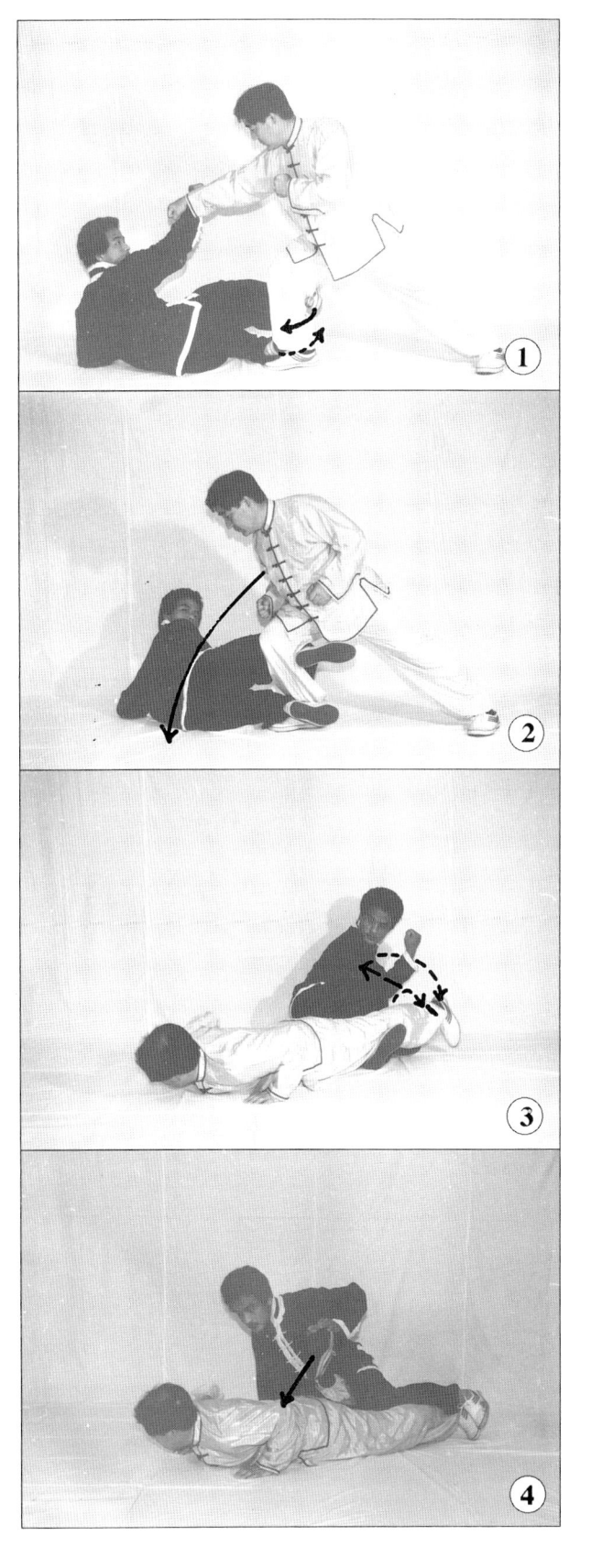

2. Golden Hooks Twist like Scissors

1) While A forms a left lying stance on the ground, **B** takes a step towards **A**'s right side with the right foot, and thrusts the right obliquely downward to attack **A**.

2) With the body slightly turning to the left, **A** stretches the left leg to hook **B**'s right leg by the ankle, and swings the right leg backward to bump against the hollow of **B**'s right knee. Both legs then twist with great strength like scissors.

3) Losing his balance, **B** is forced to fall forward.

4) A sits up and turns to the right, holding **B**'s right foot with the left hand to bend the leg. Simultaneously, the left leg swings over to press upon the calf of **B**'s left leg.

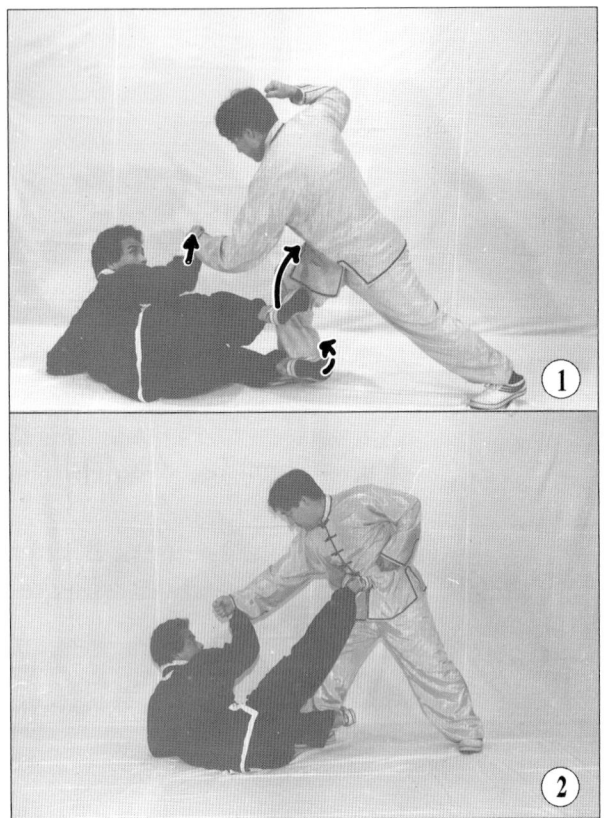

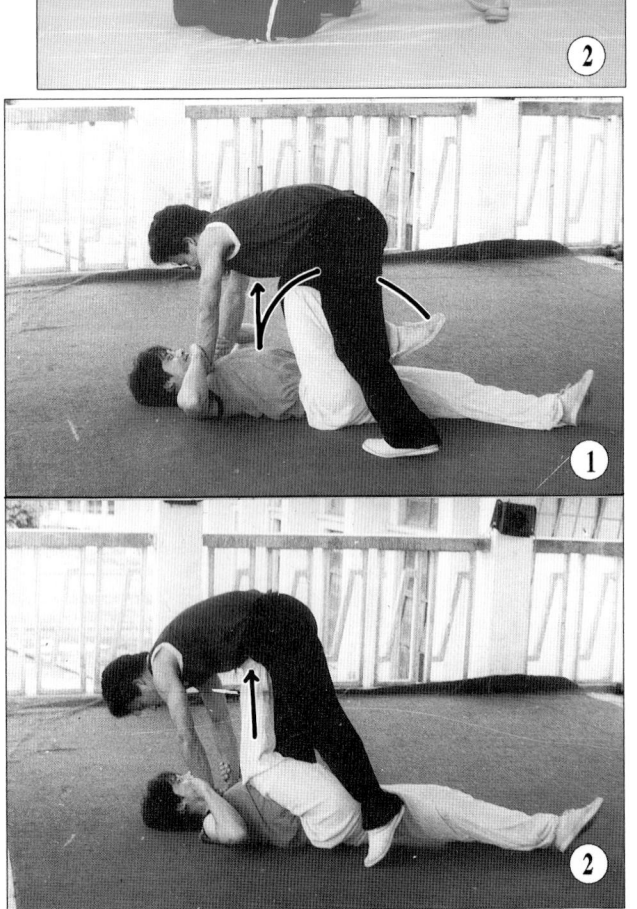

3. The Rascally Dog Stretches Its Leg

1) While **A** forms a left lying stance on the ground, **B** steps up with the right foot from the left side and smashes the right fist down.

2) **A** swings the right fist upward to block **B**'s blow and stretches the left hand out to grip **B**'s right ankle. Meanwhile, bend the left leg to hook **B**'s right foot by the heel. The right leg then kicks towards **B**'s abdomen, forcing him to fall backward.

4. The Leg towards the Sky

1) While **B** lies on his back with the right leg raised and the knee bent, **A** pounces forward to seize **B** by the throat.

2) As both hands grip **A**'s wrists and push them upward, **B** raises the right foot to kick upward on **A**'s belly, forcing him to roll forward.

5. Bumping with the Knee

1) While **B** lies on the right side of the body, **A** steps up from the right side and squats down on the right leg, with the left knee placed behind on the ground. At the same time, **A** smashes the right fist down.

2) With the left fist swings upward to block **A**'s blow, **A** turns to the right and bumps the left knee against **A**'s right flank, forcing him to fall and roll sideways.

6. The Boatman at the Helm

1) While **B** lies on his back, **A** steps up from the back and squats down on the right leg, with the left knee placed behind on the ground, seizing **B** by the throat.

2) As both hands grip **A**'s wrists and push them upward, **B** straightens the hips by pressing on the ground with the toes of the left foot. Simultaneously, **B** raises the right leg with the knee bent, and then swings the foot upward to kick **A** on the chin or on the face.

7. The Ferocious Dog Blocks the Way

1) While **A** forms a left lying stance on the ground, **B** launches a frontal attack in a right bow step.

2) As the left foot stretches out to hook **B**'s right foot by the heel, **A** raises the right leg to kick **B** on the right knee, forcing him to fall backward.

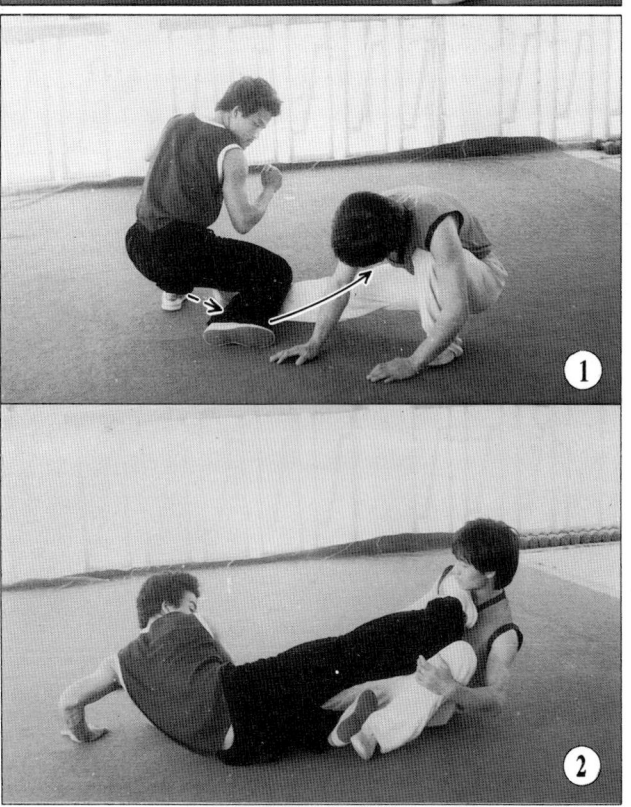

8. The Agile Dog Lies on the Ground

1) While **B** squats on the left leg and sweeps the right leg counter-clockwise, **A** crouches down to form a left single bat stance, with the right knee pressing upon **B**'s right lower leg.

2) Without any pause, **A** leans to the left so as to form a left lying stance, with both hands placed on the ground to support the torso. At the same time, **A** stretches the right leg to kick **B** on the chest or on the throat.

9. The Lying Dog Turns Over

1) While **B** forms a left lying stance on the ground, **A** steps up and raises the right foot to tread on **B**'s right knee.

2) At the same moment, **A** seizes **A**'s right foot quickly with the right hand.

3) Without any pause, **B** twists **A**'s right foot outward and swings the right leg to the right, therefore causing him to turn round to the left. After that, **B** stretches the right leg forcefully to kick **A** on the buttocks.

10. The Wily Hare Kicks with Both Legs (1)

1) Having been hit violently on the chest, **A** is forced to lean backward.

2) B immediately steps up and smashes the right fist down. At this moment, **A** falls down in a supine position, with both legs raised and the knees bent to huddle himself up.

3) With both arms and shoulders placed firmly on the ground, **A** straightens the body upward, kicking vigorously with both feet towards **B**'s chest.

11. Two Snakes Twine round the Neck (1)

1) While A forms a left (or right) lying stance on the ground, **B** launches an attack from behind.

2) A lies on his back with both hands gripping **B**'s wrists tightly, then swings the legs upward to lock **B** by the neck from both sides.

3) Without any pause, **A** swings both legs downward powerfully and then sits up, causing **B** to roll forward and throwing him onto the ground.

12. Upper Kicking and Hooking (1)

1) While A forms a left lying stance on the ground, B advances to form a left bow step and thrusts the left fist obliquely downward.

2) As the left foot stretches out to hook B's left foot by the heel, A swings the right leg upward and inward to kick B on the left arm.

3) Continuing from the preceding movement, A swings the right leg downward and outward, striking the inner side of B's left knee with the heel, the left foot still hooking B's left leg firmly, therefore causing him to fall sideways.

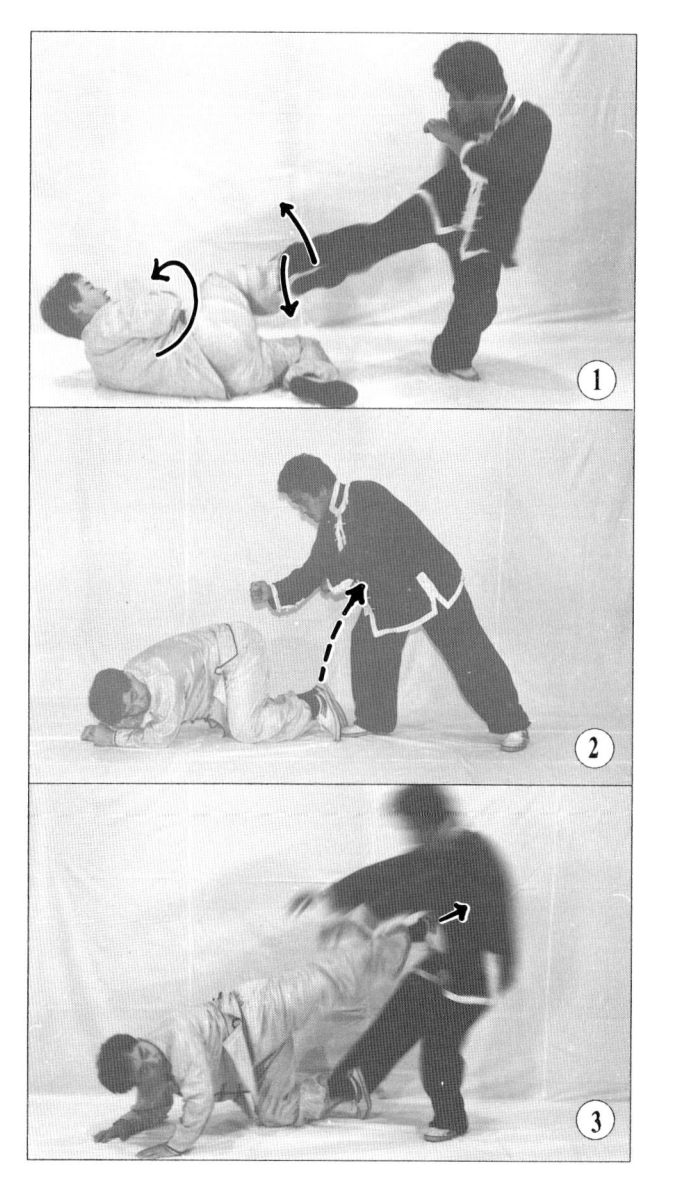

13. Tiger Tail Leg (1)

1) While B forms a left lying stance on the ground, **A** kicks forward with the right leg.

2) At this moment, **B** rolls longitudinally to the left.

3) While kneeling on the right knee with both hands placed on the ground to support the torso, **B** stretches the left leg backward to kick **A** on the belly or on the crotch.

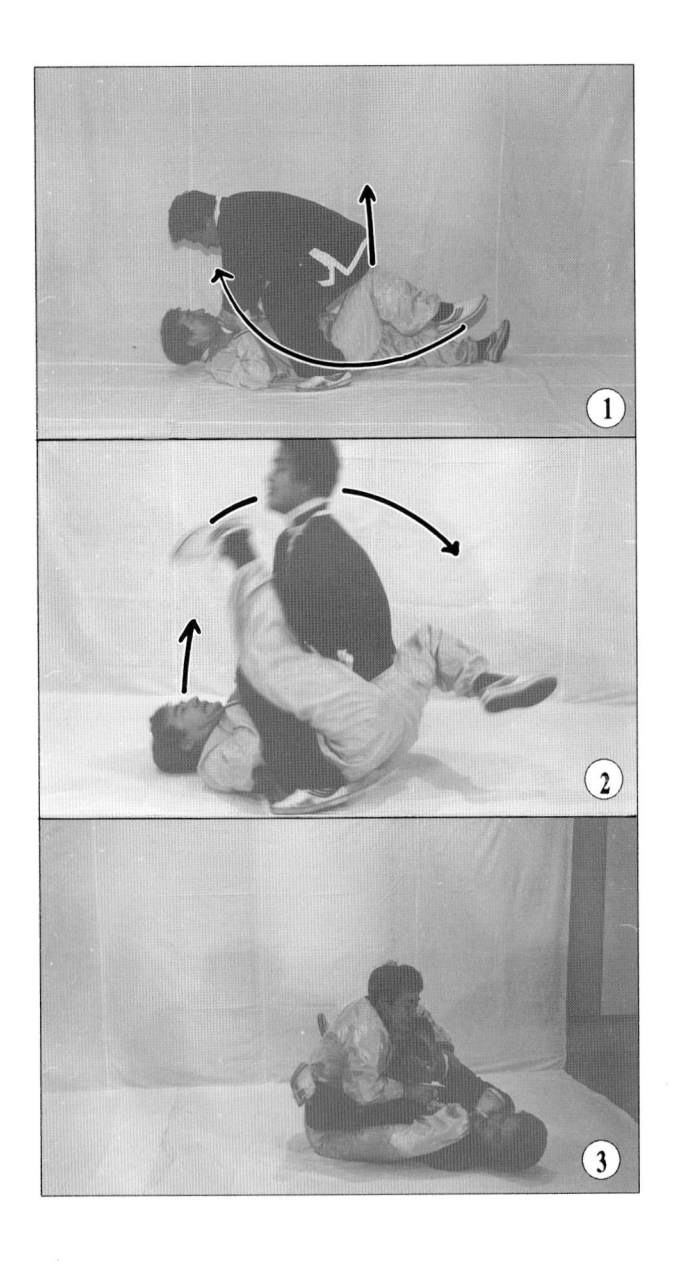

14. The Boy Sits in Meditation

1) While **B** lies on his back, **A** pounces forward to sit down on **B**'s belly and seizes **B** by the throat.

2) With both hands gripping **A**'s wrists and pushing them upward, **B** swings the right foot up to bump against **A**'s neck.

3) Without any pause, **B** sits up and presses the right foot down against **A**'s throat, causing **A** to fall backward. Both hands do not release the grip through the action.

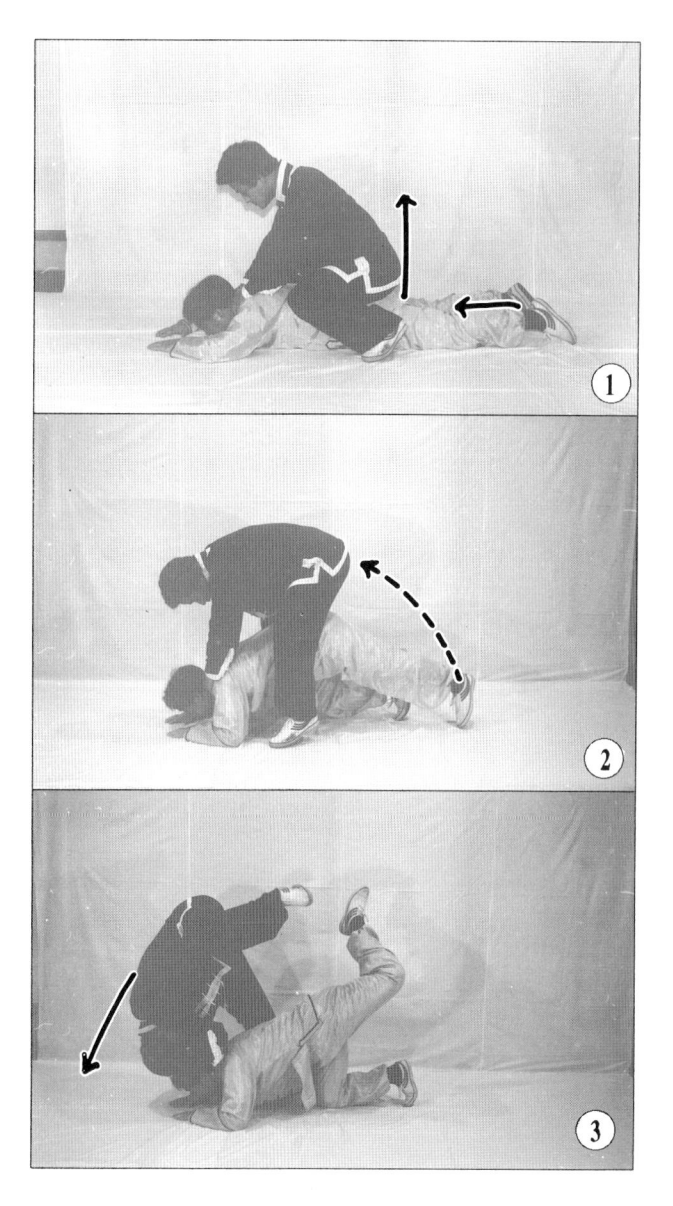

15. Kicking the Golden Incense Burner from the Back

1) While **B** takes a prostrate position on the ground, **A** pounces forward and sits on **B**'s back, with both hands seizing **B**'s shoulders.

2) At this moment, **B** arches his back by bending the hips and legs to kneel on both knees, tossing **A** upward and forward.

3) When **A** is forced to lean forward and loosen his grip, **B** suddenly lower the hips and swings the left foot backward with the knee bent to kick **A** on the buttocks.

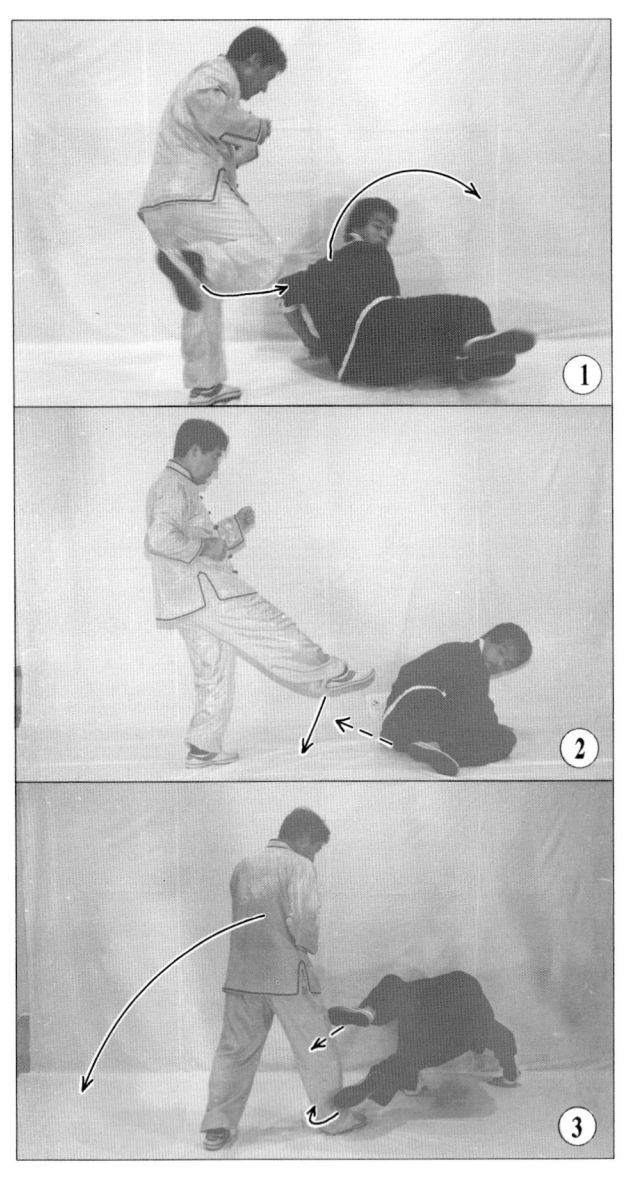

16. Turning and Piercing with Left Leg

1) While A forms a left lying stance on the ground, **B** launches an attack from the back.

2) If **B** kicks forward with the right leg, **A** sits up with both legs bent, the outer side of the left leg and the inner side of the right leg touching the ground, so as to form a left crouching bat stance.

3) Without any pause, **A** props himself up by pushing the ground with both hands. The torso then leans to the right to form a right lying stance. Meanwhile, the left leg pierces sideways to kick **B** on the right knee.

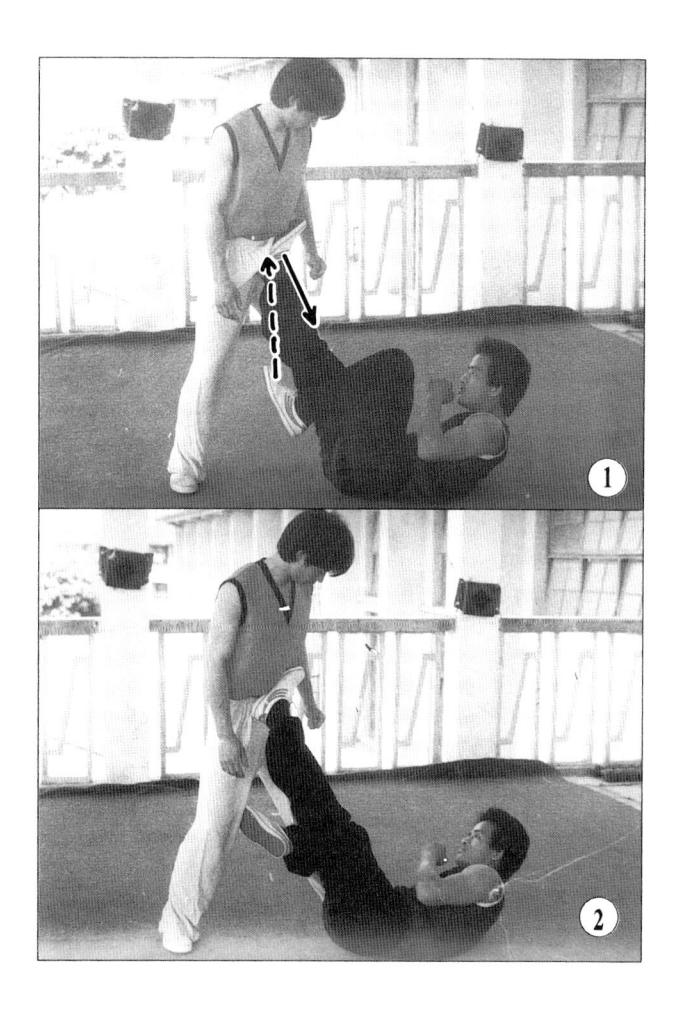

17. Serial Kicking

1) **B** falls backward on his own initiative, with the left leg bent and the right leg raised to kick upward on **A**'s belly. The right hand grips **A**'s left ankle tightly in the meantime.

2) Without any pause, **B** lower the right foot by bending the knee and presses the right leg against **A**'s left knee/ Simultaneously, B raises the left leg to kick upward on **A**'s belly. The right hand pulls **A**'s left foot up in the meantime, thus forcing him to fall backward. (In this figure, **B** is dressed in black and **A** in white.)

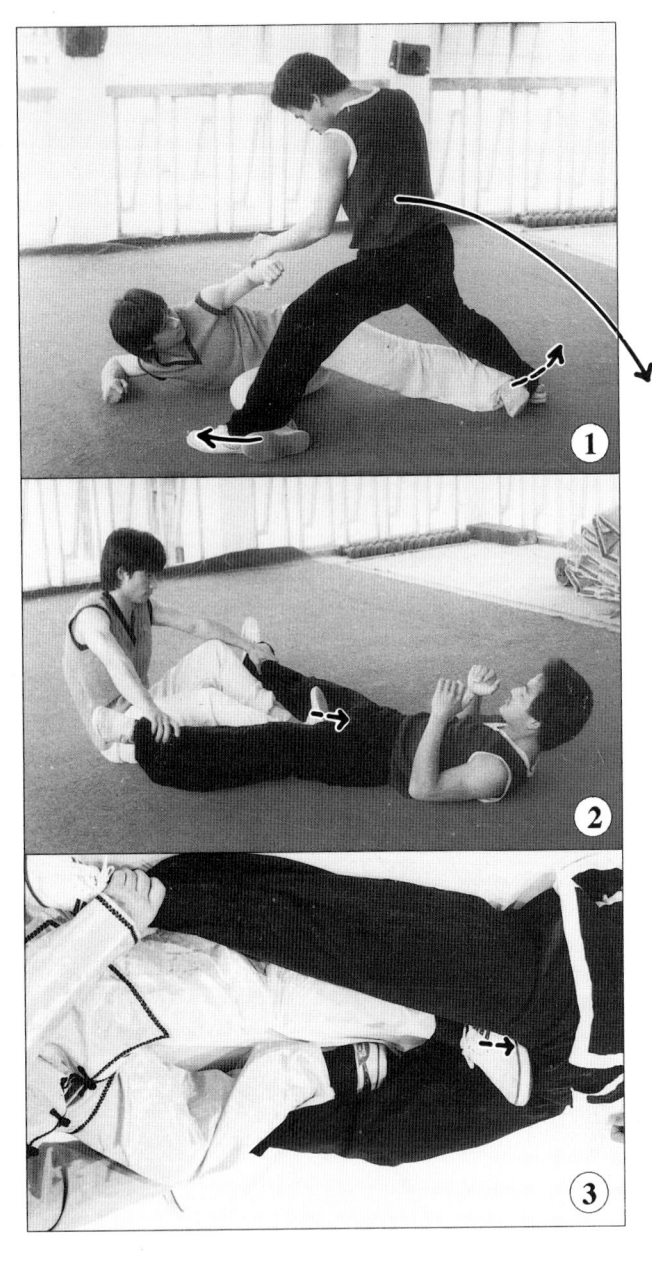

18. Separating Legs

1) **B** falls sideways down on his own initiative and slides forward on the ground. Meanwhile, separate the legs. The right leg sweeps up to hook **A**'s left foot by the heel; while the left leg stretches to bump against the inner side of **A**'s right foot, thus throwing **A** into an unbalanced position with the feet extremely widened.

2) **B** immediately sits up with both hands gripping **A**'s ankles and pulling them back, therefore causing him to fall backward. Then, with the right leg still pressing against **A**'s left leg, **B** stretches the left leg to kick **A** on the crotch.

19. Burning Joss Sticks to the Heavens

1) While **B** thrusts the right fist straight ahead or swings the right fist forward from the side, **A** takes a step forward with the left foot and swings the left hand forward to makes a grab at **B**'s right arm.

2) Without any pause, **A** falls backward on his own initiative with the left leg bent. As the left hand drops to grip **B**'s right ankle, the right leg kicks upward on **B**'s crotch with the heel.

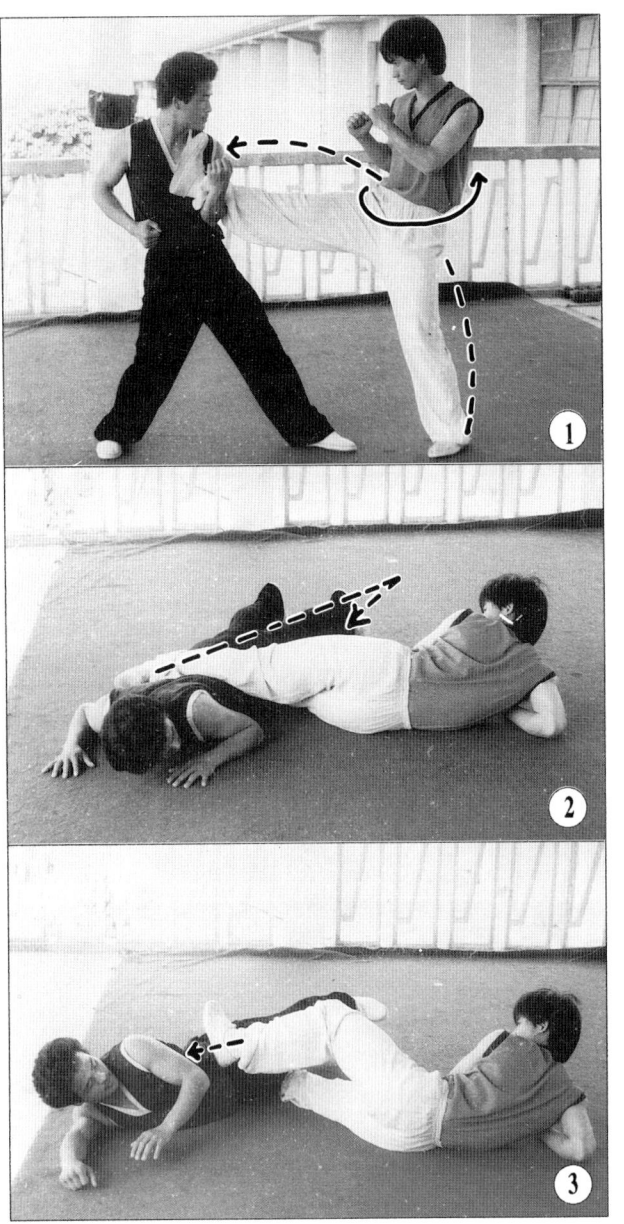

20. The Heavenly Dog Rolls a Ball

1) While **B** kicks straight ahead with the heel of the right foot, **A** hugs **B**'s right leg up with the left arm.

2) At the very moment, **B** turns round to the left an swings the left leg upward and backward, striking **A** on the back with the heel. Both legs twist powerfully like scissors, causing **A** to fall in a prostrate position onto the ground. While turning round, **B** drops down on the right side of the body, with both hands placed on the ground to support the torso.

3) Without any pause, **B** raises his left leg to kick **A** on the waist, forcing him to roll longitudinally round.

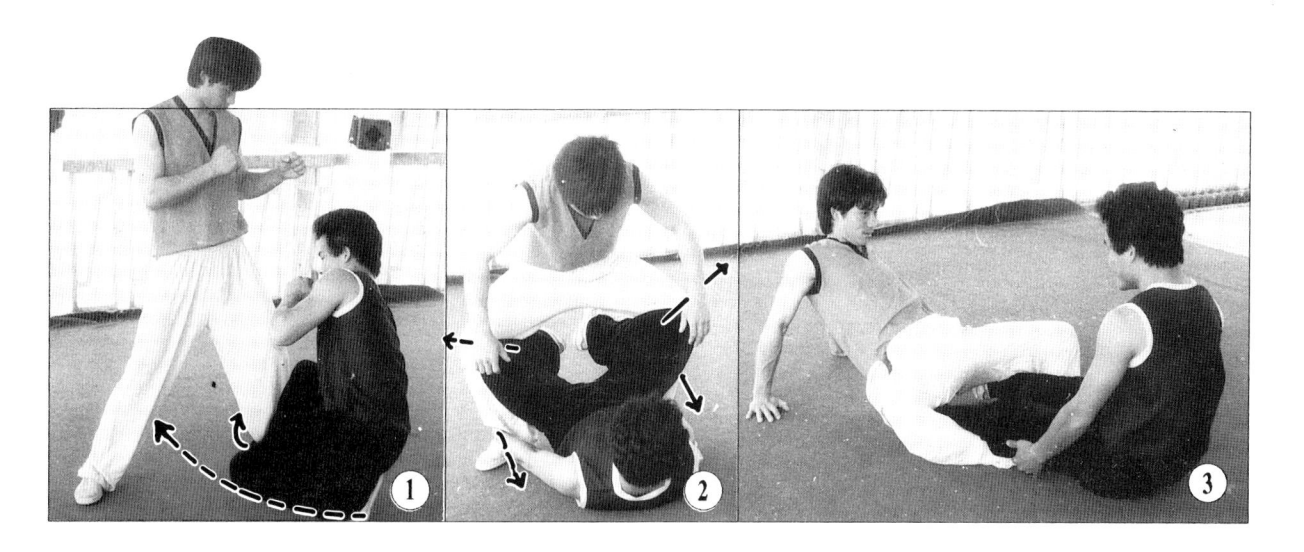

21. Buddha Guanyin Descends to the World

1) While both sides stand upright confronting each other or thrusting fists at the opponent, **A** makes a feint of an offensive on his own initiative, and then squats down quickly, pressing against **B**'s left lower leg from the inside with the right leg and seizing **B**'s left ankle with the right hand.

2) Without any pause, **A** leans to the left and falls down with the left shoulder first touching the ground. Meanwhile, insert the left leg to press against **B**'s right leg and grip **B**'s right ankle with the left hand. With both knees widely opened, both hands then press inward in order to bend **B**'s legs and make him drop down.

3) When **B** is forced to sit down, **A** sits up, stiffening both legs to prize **B**'s thighs up. Both hands push **B**'s feet inward to lock them under the legs in the meantime.

22. Lower Kicking and Hooking

1) While both sides stand upright confronting each other, **A** falls backward onto the ground on his own initiative and slides forward, with the left leg bent and the right leg raised to kick **B** on the belly. The left hand grips **B**'s right ankle in the meantime.

2) Without any pause, **A** turns slightly to the left. As the left foot hooks **B**'s right leg by the ankle, the right leg swings to the left and pierces through the space under **B**'s crotch to kick **B** on the inner side of his left knee, therefore causing him to turn to the left and fall sideways down.

3) Continuing from the preceding movement, **A** sits up, with the left hand still controlling **B**'s right ankle.

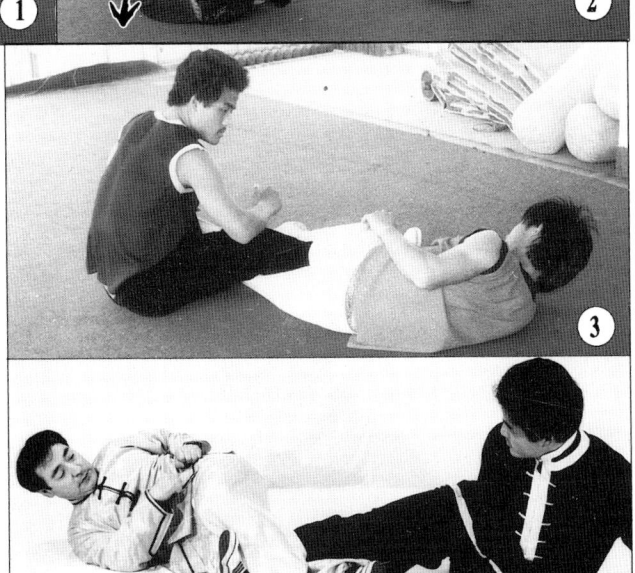

86

23. Threading a Needle

1) While **B** kicks straight ahead with the right leg, **A** hugs **B**'s right leg up with the right arm.

2) At the very moment, **B** falls down with the left side of the body touching the ground, the left foot sliding forward to bump against the heel of **A**'s left foot.

3) Without any pause, **B** turns to the left and swings the right leg upward to kick **A** on the throat, causing him to fall backward.

24. Two Snakes Twine round the Neck (2)

1) **B** grips **A**'s right wrist with both hands and twists the arm outward.

2) Following **B**'s twisting force, **A** turns to the left and falls down on his back under **B**'s crotch, with both hands conversely gripping **B**'s wrists tightly in front of the chest. Meanwhile, **A** swings the legs upward to lock **B** by the neck from both sides.

3) Without any pause, **A** swings the legs downward powerfully with both ankles still gripping **B**'s neck firmly, therefore causing **B** to roll forward and throwing him onto the ground. Both hands do not release the grip until the body sits up.

25. Tiger Tail Leg (2)

1) While both sides stand upright confronting each other, **B** raises the right foot to tread on **A**'s left knee.

2) Having been hit by **B**'s right foot, **A** swiftly turns to the right and squats down on the right leg, with the left knee knelt on the ground.

3) Without any pause, **A** continues to turn to the right and places both hands on the ground to support the torso. Meanwhile, the right leg kicks backward and upward on **B**'s belly.

26. The General Dismounts from a Horse

1) While B thrusts the right fist straight ahead, **A** swings the left hand forward to make a grab at **B**'s right arm.

2) Without any pause, **A** squat down quickly, with the right knee placed behind on the ground and the left knee pressing against **B**'s left leg. Hold the left arm crosswise in front of the chest with the elbow bent. Meanwhile, the right hand grips **B**'s left foot and draws it back, causing **B** to fall backward.

27. Backward Hooking

1) **B** grips **A**'s right arm with both hands and twists it behind **A**'s back. Following the twisting force, **A** turns to the left with the back towards the opponent.

2) Continuing from the turning movement, **A** kneels down on the left knee with the left hand placed on the ground to support the torso. Meanwhile, the right leg swings backward and upward with the knee slightly bent, striking **B** on the crotch with the heel.

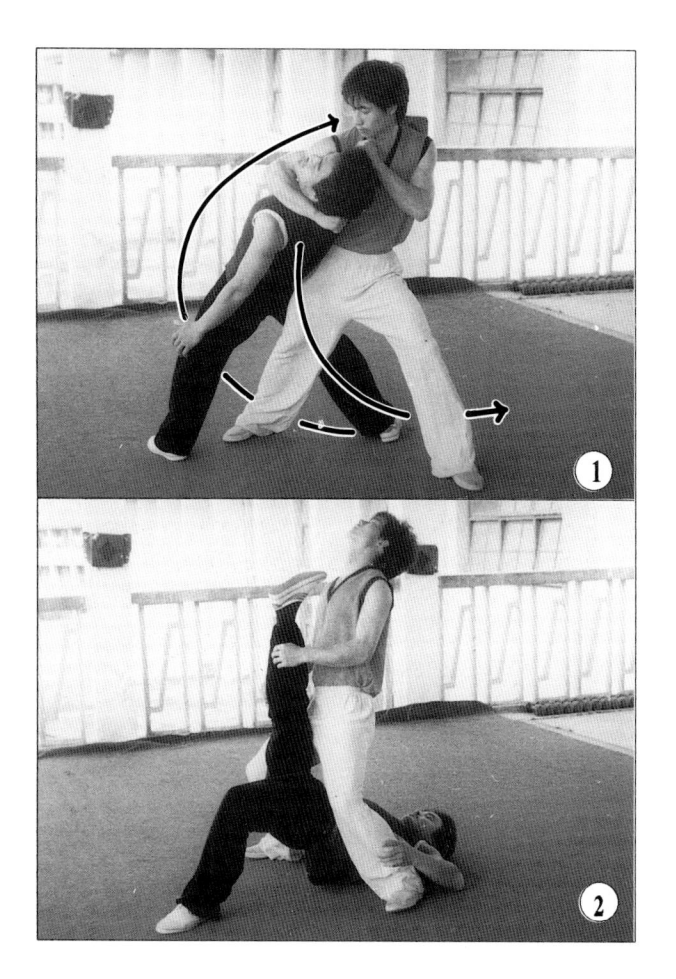

28. Frontal Kicking with the Hooked Foot

1) While inserting the right leg behind **A**, **B** swings the right arm forward round **A**'s neck in order to knock him over.

2) Following **B**'s attacking force, **A** falls down on his back and then penetrates ahead through the space under **B**'s crotch. Simultaneously, with the right foot pressing on the ground to straighten the hips, the left leg kicks upward on **B**'s throat with the foot tightly hooked. Both hands clasp **B**'s ankles in the meantime.

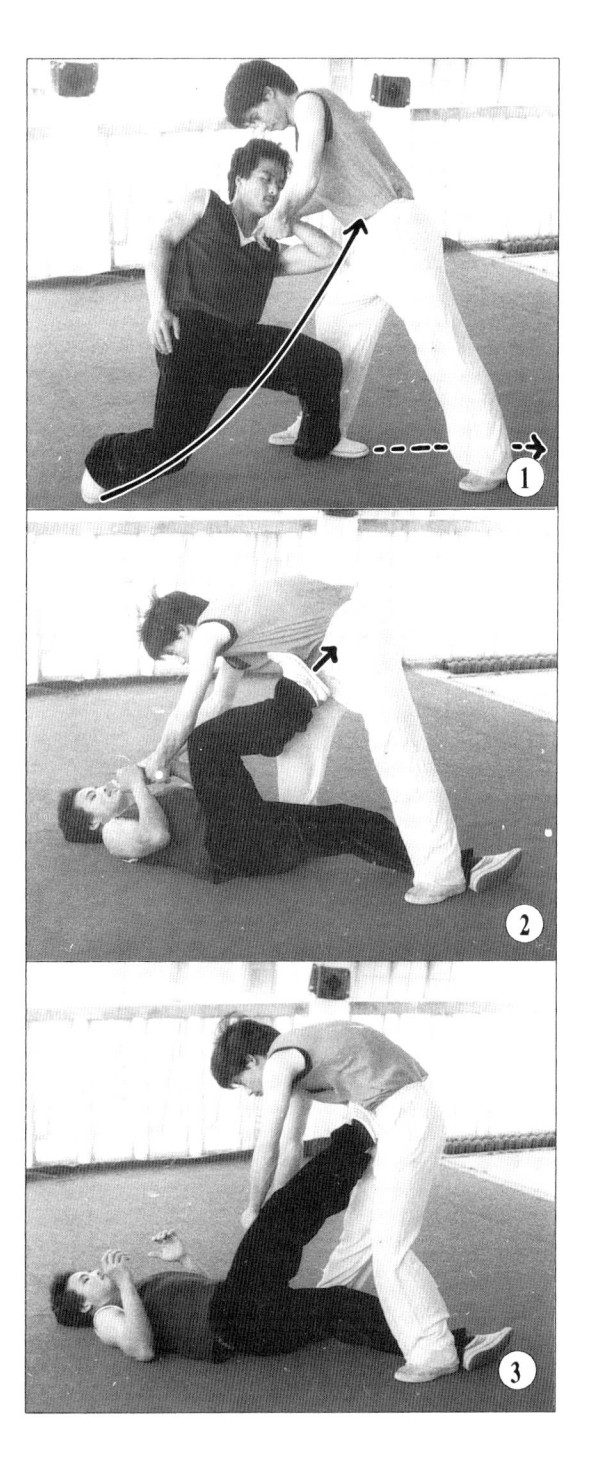

29. The Rascally Dog Kicks with Its Heel Three Times

1) **B** grips **A**'s right wrist with both hands and bend the joint with great strength, forcing **A** to sink to the ground.

2) At the very moment, **A** falls down on his back, with the left foot sliding forward on the ground under **B**'s crotch. As the body falls, **A** raises the right foot to bump against B's belly, and wrenches **B**'s hands forcefully with the right hand so as to extricate the left hand from **B**'s hold.

3) Without any pause, **A** stretches the right leg to kick upward. If **B** remains standing, give him two more kicks with the left leg and the right leg in sequence.

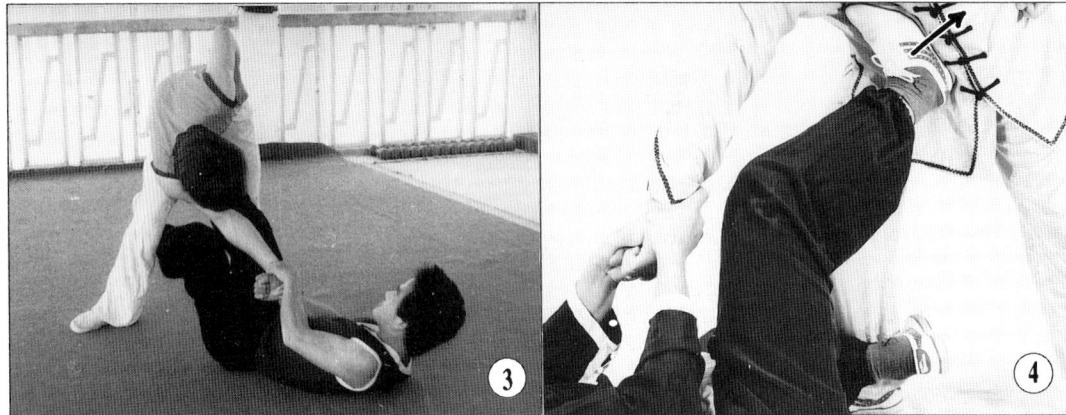

30. The Agile Dog Turns Its Belly Over

1) While both sides stand upright confronting each other, **B** stretches his right hand out to grip **A**'s right wrist.

2) As the left foot takes a step to the right front, **A** crouches down and turns to the right with the right leg bent and the knee placed on the ground. Meanwhile, with the left hand gripping **B**'s right wrist tightly, both hands twist **B**'s right arm outward.

3) While the body continues to turn to the right, **A** lies on his back, with both hands still controlling **B**'s right arm, thus forcing **B** to bow down. Meanwhile, with the left foot hooking **B**'s right leg by the hollow of the knee, **A** raises the right foot to kick **B** on the belly.

94

31. The Monkey Climbs a Tree

1) While **B** swings both fists forward from both sides to strike **A** on the ears, **A** raises both hands to block the blow.

2) Without any pause, **A** jumps up and hooks both legs around **B**'s waist. Meanwhile, the torso drops down onto the ground, with both hands seizing **B**'s legs by the heels.

3) Continuing from the preceding movement, **A** bends the legs and sets the feet against **B**'s belly.

4) Without any pause, **A** stretches both legs forcefully to kick upward. Both hands loosen the grip in the meantime.

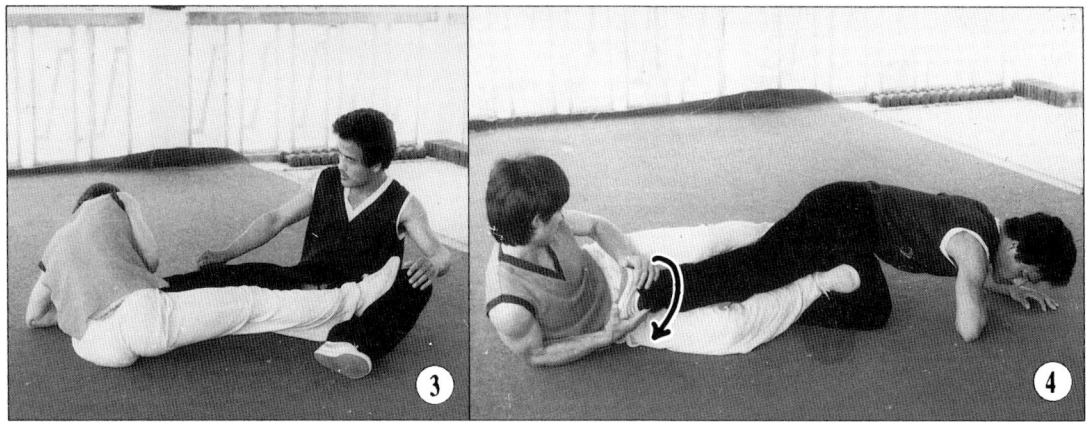

32. Single-line Leg

1) While **A** thrusts the right fist straight ahead, **B** grips **A**'s right arm with both hands and presses it down to ward off the attack.

2) Without any pause, **B** leaps forward and falls sideways down. With the left leg bent to hook **A**'s right leg by the heel, the right foot slides forward on the ground to push **A**'s left foot away, thus throwing **A** into an unbalanced position with the feet extremely widened.

3) When **A** is forced to sit down on the ground, **B** raises the right foot to kick **A** on the left knee and clasps **A**'s right foot with both hands.

4) Without any pause, **B** twists **A**'s right foot inward so as to turn him over. The right foot bumps against **A**'s crotch in the meantime.

33. The Lying Dragon Wags Its Tail

1) While **A** stands upright with legs together, **B** clasps **A**'s lower legs from the back with both arms and butts his shoulder against **A**'s buttocks.

2) As **A** is forced to fall forward onto the ground, **B** inserts his right foot forward between **A**'s legs.

3) At this moment, **A** turns to the right swiftly, sweeping the left leg forward and swinging the right leg horizontally backward. Both legs twist like scissors, causing **B** to fall sideways down.

4) Continuing from the preceding movement, **A** immediately sits up. With the left foot pressing upon the hollow of **B**'s left knee, both hands grip **B**'s right foot, then bend the leg and wrench the foot outward.

97

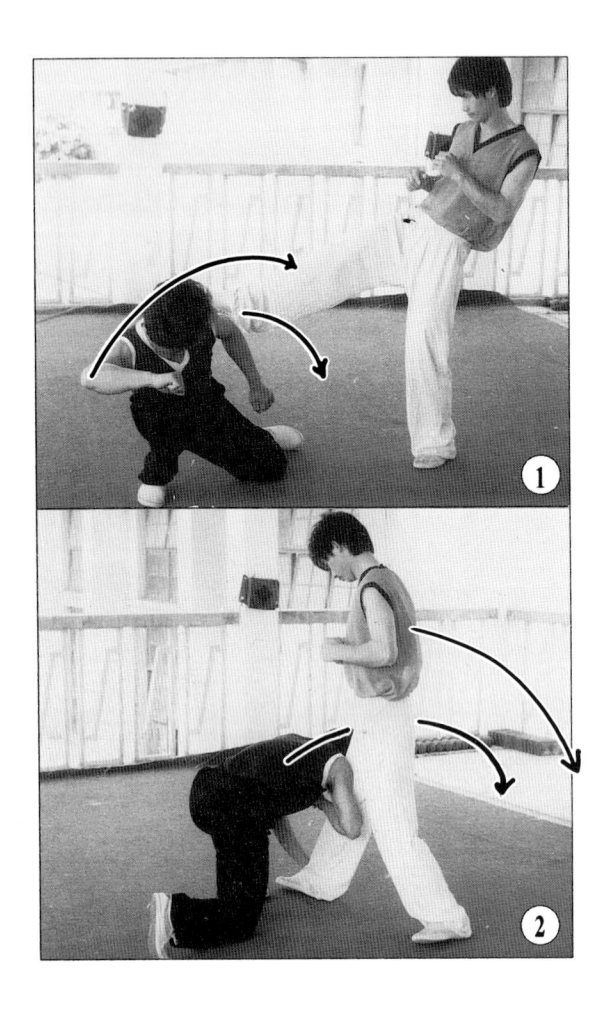

34. The Hungry Dog Springs on the Meat

1) When **B** kicks forward with his right leg, **A** squat down on the right leg with the left knee placed on the ground to form a right single bat stance, so as to dodge **B**'s attack.

2) Immediately after **B**'s right foot lands on the ground, **A** springs forward with the right forearm held crosswise in front of the chest to press against **B**'s right knee. The left hand grips **B**'s right foot by the heel in the meantime.

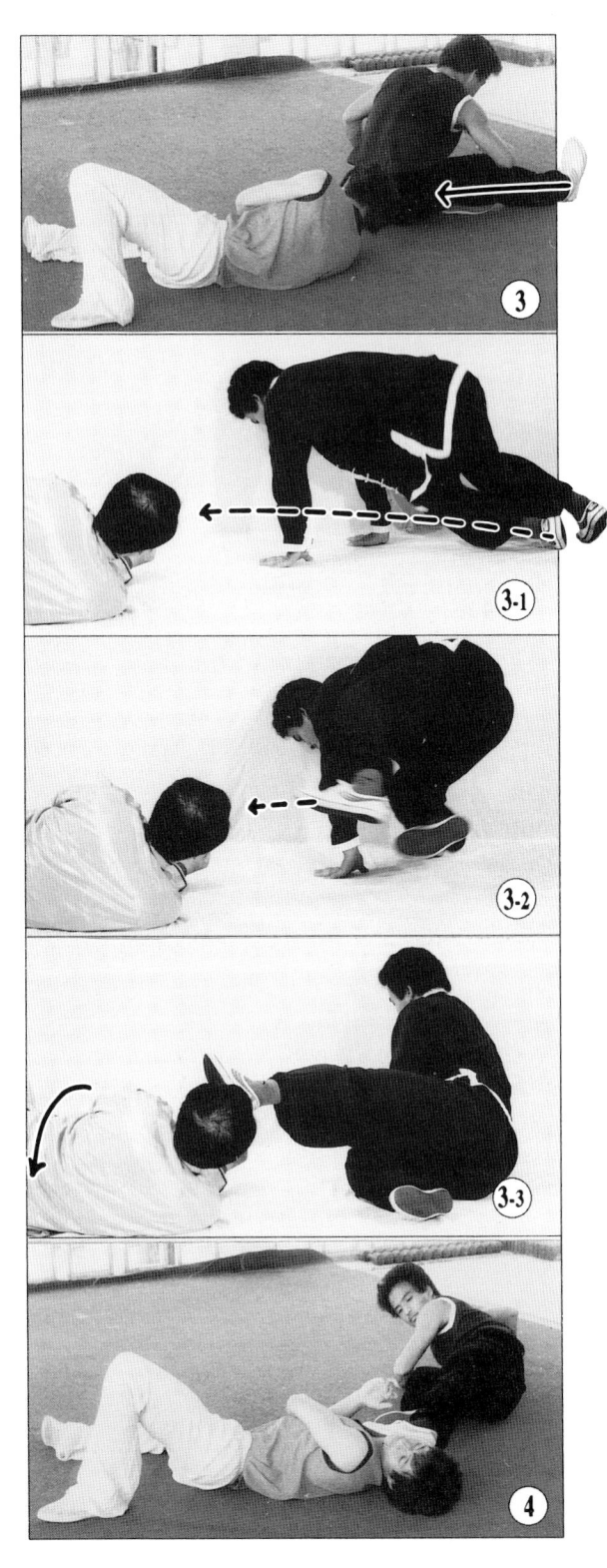

98

3) Having lost his balance, **B** is forced to fall sideways down. Simultaneously, **A** performs a shoulder roll and then sits up.

4) Without any pause, **A** turns round from the left with both hands placed on the ground to support the torso. Then, with the right leg bent and its outer side touching the ground, **A** stretches the left leg to kick **B** on the throat.

35. The Wily Hare Kicks with Both Legs (2)

1) While **A** stands upright with legs together, **B** clasp **A**'s lower legs from the front with both arms and butts his shoulder against **A**'s belly.

2) Following **B**'s wrestling force, **A** falls backward, with the buttocks first touching the ground, and then the back and the shoulder. Meanwhile, **A** bends the hips and the legs to huddle himself up, with the chin slightly drawn in so as to fix the eyes on the opponent.

3) Without any pause, with both arms and shoulders placed firmly on the ground, **A** straightens the body up, kicking vigorously with the feet towards **B**'s chest.

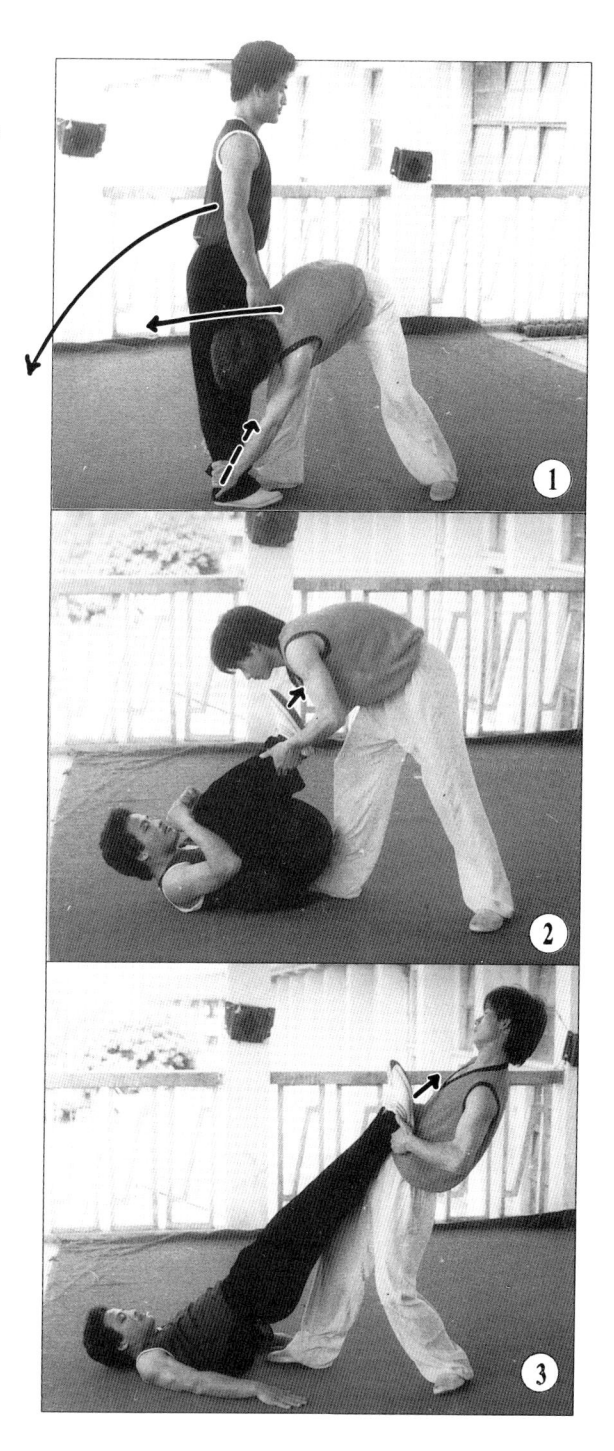

36. The Black Dog Wags Its Tail

1) When losing the upper-level fighting, **B** falls backward onto the ground with the left leg bent and the right leg raised to kick upward.

2) While **A** gets close and twists **B**'s right foot outward with both hands, **B** turns to the right, swinging the left leg upward and inward to strike **A** on the right flank.

37. The Rascal Takes Off His Boot

1) While **B** lies on his back, **A** pounces forward from the right and squat down on the left leg, with the right knee placed behind on the ground, in order to seize **B** by the throat. As **A** bows down, **B** raises the right foot to bump against **A**'s belly.

2) Without any pause, **B** stretches the right leg to kick upward with great strength.

38. The Bat Perches on the Ground

1) **B** inserts his arms under **A**'s armpits from the back, and then raises the arms until both hands overlap on the back of **A**'s neck, so as to lock **A**'s arms and control **A**'s head.

2) To extricate himself from such a predicament, **A** suddenly kneels down with the thighs together and the heels apart to form a double bat stance. At the same time, **A** raises both hands to seize **B** by the neck.

3) Continuing from the preceding movement, **A** bows down, causing **B** to roll forward, and then throws him onto the ground.

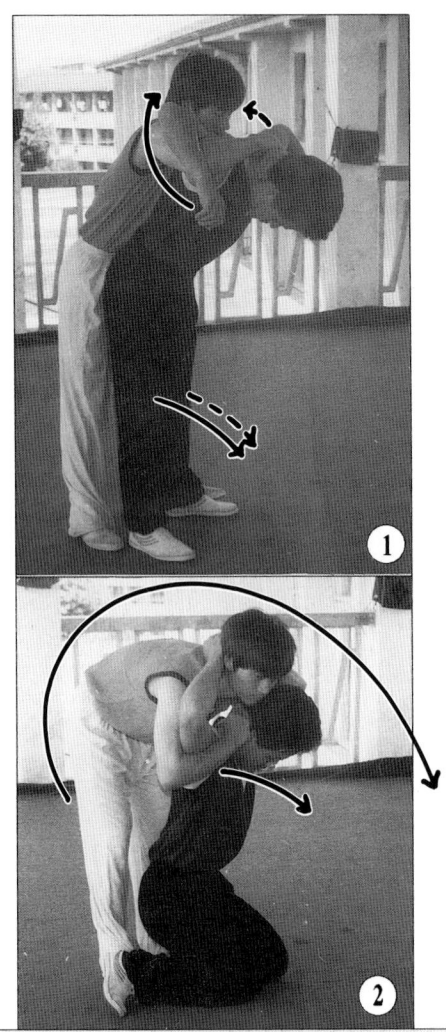

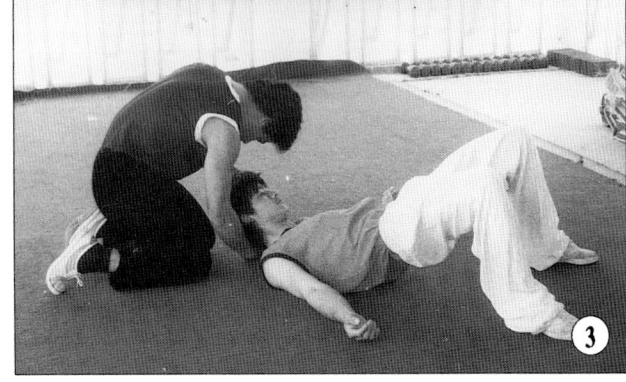

39. The Drunken Dog Lies on the Ground

1) While **B** thrusts his right fist straight ahead, **A** swiftly shift the weight backward to dodge **B**'s blow.

2) Without any pause, **A** falls down to the right side, with the right foot sliding forward on the ground to push **B**'s right foot and the left leg bent at the knee to support the body. As the body falls, with the right hand gripping **B**'s right wrist and the left hand holding the elbow, both hands exert strength to pull **B** down.

3) While loosening his grip, **A** raises the left foot to kick **B** on the belly with the heel.

40. The Old Man Pulls a Cart

1) **B** clasps **A**'s waist from the back with both arms and inserts the right leg under **A**'s crotch.

2) **A** sits down on **B**'s right knee, with both hands gripping **B**'s right foot and pulling it upward, therefore causing **B** to fall backward onto the ground.

3) At this moment, **A** raises the left foot to kick **A** on the buttocks, causing him to roll forward. The right leg draws back with the knee bent in the meantime.

press against **B**'s knees from the inside, with both hands gripping **B**'s ankles and pushing the feet inward.

3) Continuing from the preceding movement, **A** raises the right foot to kick **B** on the buttocks, with the left foot hooking **B**'s left leg by the knee and both the hands pulling **B**'s feet backward.

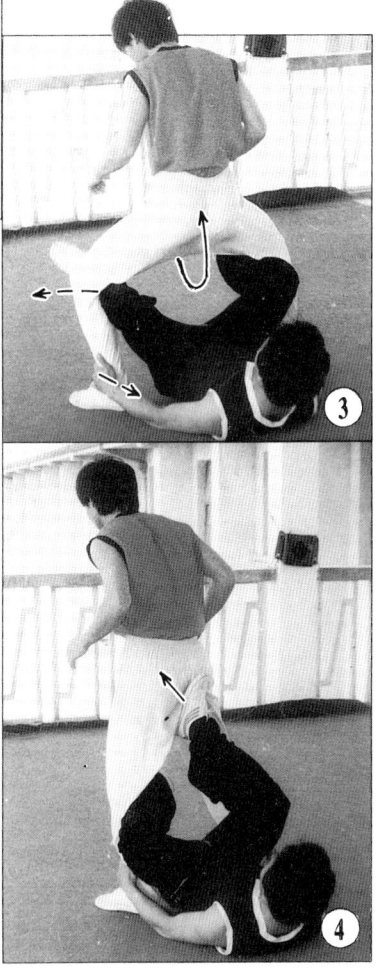

41. The Agile Dog Penetrates under the Crotch

1) When **B** kicks forward with the left leg, **A** moves the left foot to the left front and inclines the torso to the left so as to dodge **B**'s attack. Meanwhile, the right arm swings outward to ward off **B**'s left leg.

2) Without any pause, **A** takes a step forward with the right foot, and falls down with the right shoulder first touching the ground. The body then penetrates forward through the space under **B**'s crotch. While lying on the back, **A** bends the legs to

42. The Carp Tosses in Seething Waves

1) When **B** thrusts his right fist straight ahead with the right leg in front, **A** takes a step forward with the right foot, and swings the right hand forward to make a grab at **B**'s right arm.

2) Without any pause, **A** moves his right foot further ahead to form a right bow step on the right side of **B**'s body, with both hands gripping **B**'s right wrist and twisting the arm to the back. The torso turns to the left and penetrates forward under **B**'s right arm while the right foot advances.

3) As the torso continues to turn to the left, **A** lies down on his back, with the left foot hooking **B**'s right leg by the shin and the right foot bumping against **B**'s waist. Both hands keep on twisting **B**'s right arm so as to throw him over.

43. The Dog Bites a Rice Dumpling

1) When **B** thrusts his right fist straight ahead in a right bow step, **A** advances with the right foot and swings the right hand forward to make a grab at **B**'s attacking arm.

2) Without any pause, **A** takes a step forward with the left foot, and then falls behind **B**'s legs with the left side of the body touching the ground. As the body goes down, twist **B**'s right arm to his back with the right hand. At the same time, **A** stretches the left leg through the space under **B**'s crotch to hook **B**'s right leg by the shin, and raises the right leg with the knee bent to bump against **B**'s buttocks. The left arm locks **B**'s left leg by the ankle from the inside in the meantime.

3) Without any pause, **A** stretches the right leg forcefully to kick **B** on the buttocks, causing him to fall forward.

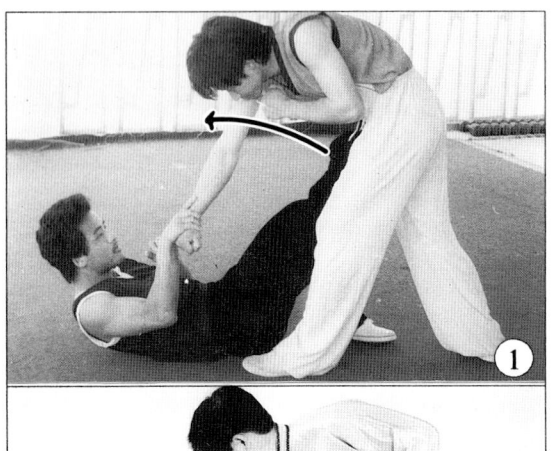

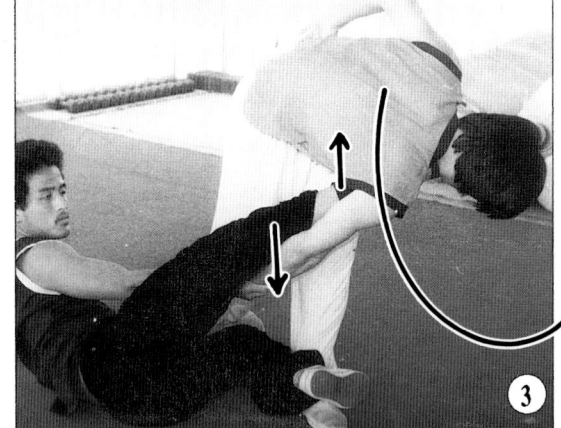

44. Upper Kicking and Hooking (2)

1) When **B** thrusts his right fist straight ahead or stretches the right hand forward in order to seize **A** by the throat, **A** falls down and slides forward on his own initiative, both hands taking a firm grip on

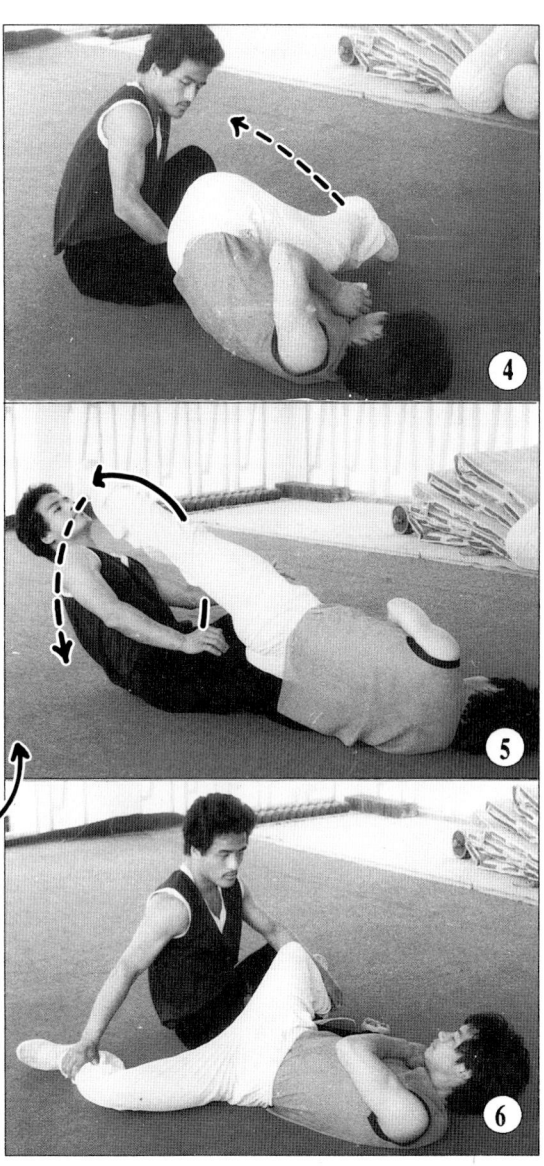

B's right wrist and pulling the arm down. At the same time, with the left leg bent and the foot placed on the ground, **A** raises the right foot to kick upward on **B**'s belly.

2) Continuing from the preceding movement, **A** turns slightly to the left. As the left leg stretches to hook **B**'s left leg by the ankle, the right leg swings across **B**'s right arm and then penetrates from under **B**'s right armpit. Thus, **B** is forced to turn to the left.

3) With the right leg pressing down, **A** sits up, forcing **B** to roll and fall sideways onto the ground.

4) If **B** sweeps his left leg backward to strike **A** on the face when he lies on the ground, **A** leans backward to dodge the blow.

5) When **B**'s left leg goes to the left side, **A** sits up again and firmly grips **B**'s ankles respectively with both hands.

45. The Celestial Binding

1) **B** takes a step forward with his right foot, and seizes **A** by the throat with his right hand.

2) At the very moment, **A** falls backward on his own initiative. As the right foot slides forward on the ground to push **B**'s right foot away, both hands grip **B**'s right arm and pull it down, therefore throwing **B** into an unbalanced position. Meanwhile, **A** raises the left foot to kick **B** on the chest.

3) Continuing from the preceding movement, **A** lowers the left foot to hook **B**'s right foot up and seizes the ankle with the left hand. The right leg sweeps outward to bump against **B**'s left ankle in the meantime. While **B** is forced to drop onto the ground, **A** stretches the left leg to kick **B** on the crotch and raises the right foot to tread on the hollow of **B**'s left knee.

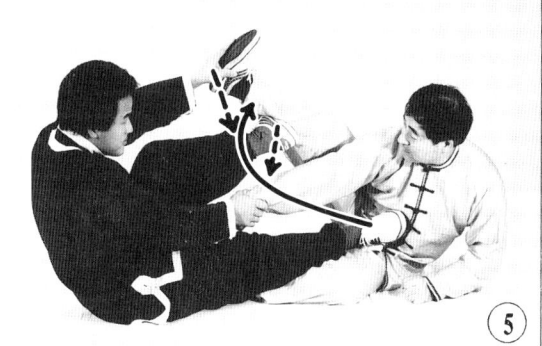

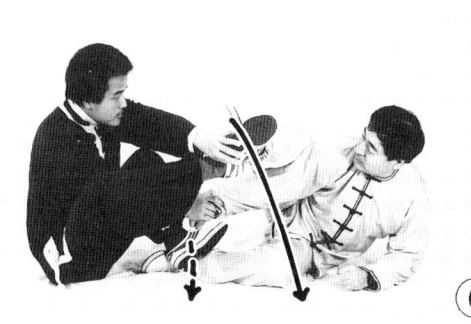

4) While sitting up, **A** grips **B**'s right foot with the left hand and wrenches the leg across **B**'s right arm to the right side. Then, **A** draws his right foot back and sets the sole firmly upon the instep of **B**'s right foot.

5) Without any pause, **A** stands up swiftly, with both hands gripping **B**'s right arm to draw it upward with great strength, as though tying him up; thus **B** is brought under **A**'s control and can not move any longer.

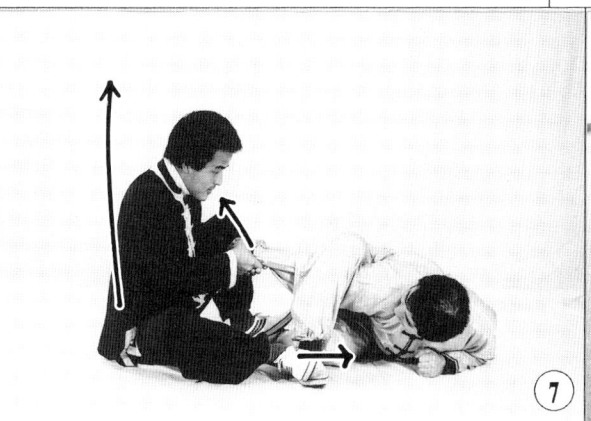

We want to help, your martial arts become more wide and deep !
Now

Chinese Martial Arts Series

Vol. 1 **T'ai Chi Ch'uan**

— **The Basic Exercises**

by Xing Yanling

Vol. 2 **T'ai-chi Swordplay** and **Eight-diagram Palm**

by Xing Yanling

Vol. 3 **Chen Style T'ai Chi Ch'uan**

— **Thirty-six and Fifty-six Movements**

by Xing Yanling

Vol. 4 **Fukien Ground Boxing**

— **Nan Shaolin Leg Techniques**

by Cai Chuxian